Rust In Practice

A Programmers Guide to Build Rust Programs, Test Applications and Create Cargo Packages

Rustacean Team

Contents

Preface

Rust In Practice is an ultimate fast-paced guide for anyone looking to become a practitioner of the rust programming from day 1. This book covers everything from the basics of Rust programming to building robust and efficient applications.

Starting with the fundamentals, this book guides you through the syntax and semantics of the Rust language, including its unique ownership model and type system. You'll learn about common data types, control flow, error handling, and more.

As you progress through the book, you'll dive deeper into advanced topics such as building programs, rust libraries and crates, using the standard library, and working with external crates. You'll also learn how to write concurrent and parallel code, take advantage of Rust's built-in testing features, and use popular Rust frameworks and libraries.

The book also provides hands-on examples and exercises to help you practice and apply the concepts you've learned. By the end of this book, you'll have a solid understanding of Rust programming and be well-equipped to start building your own robust and efficient applications. With clear explanations, practical examples, and expert advice, this book will help you get an edge on Rust programming and become proficient in building and testing Rust applications, right from day one.

In this book you will learn how to:

- Get well versed with cargo, different cargo commands
- Understanding data types, ownership, and borrowing
- Write flexible, efficient code with traits and generics
- Make use of closures, iterators, and asynchronous programming to write multi-threaded programs
- Utilizing collections, strings, text, input and output, macros, and avoiding unsafe codes
- Run code testing on different types of rust programs and applications
- 50+ examples covered to demonstrate every feature and functionality of rust

This book is written by a team of Rust professionals with an intent to contribute and return back to both industry and academic research communities.

GitforGits

Prerequisites

This book assumes you are absolutely new to rust programming and believes in rust to make some of the great performing applications. If you know any other programming prior to this book, reading this book at speed can finish truly in a day.

Rust is a modern, safe and efficient systems programming language that is widely used in industry and is a good choice for developers who want to build high-performance, concurrent, and safe systems.

Codes Usage

Are you in need of some helpful code examples to assist you in your programming and documentation? Look no further! Our book offers a wealth of supplemental material, including code examples and exercises.

Not only is this book here to aid you in getting your job done, but you have our permission to use the example code in your programs and documentation. However, please note that if you are reproducing a significant portion of the code, we do require you to contact us for permission.

But don't worry, using several chunks of code from this book in your program or answering a question by citing our book and quoting example code does not require permission. But if you do choose to give credit, an attribution typically includes the title, author, publisher, and ISBN. For example, "Rust In Practice by the Rustacean Team".

If you are unsure whether your intended use of the code examples falls under fair use or the permissions outlined above, please do not hesitate to reach out to us at kittenpub.kdp@gmail.com.

We are happy to assist and clarify any concerns.

Acknowledgement

The Rustacean team would express their gratitude to all of the other contributors to Rust and work tirelessly to improve the quality of the programming language. While they are doing this, they would want to express their gratitude to the copywriters, tech editors, and reviewers who helped create a powerful yet simple book that outperforms rust coding in a relatively short period of time.

Chapter 1: Understanding Why Rust!

Why to Learn Rust Programming?

Rust, a powerful tool that has a lot of potential that hasn't been fully realised yet, is available to those who are interested in programming and puts a lot of power in their hands. Rust is a low-level language, which means that programmes written in it are close to the hardware of the system and have the ability to produce code that is highly efficient. This is because Rust was designed to be a general-purpose, general-purpose programming language. Rust offers exceptional performance, with code that, on average, runs noticeably faster when compared to code written in other languages.

Rust offers robust memory and data safety guarantees, which means that programmes written in Rust have a lower risk of containing errors that are brought on by improper memory access. Rust is a general-purpose programming language that was designed to be used for a wide range of applications. Because finding and fixing bugs can be time-consuming and expensive work, this could help developers save both time and money.

Rust also has many modern features, such as support for asynchronous programming, which is an aspect of application development that is becoming an increasingly important component. Rust is a modern programming language that includes many modern features. In addition to this, it offers helpful tools for debugging and profiling, both of which contribute to the significantly improved smoothness of the development process.

In conclusion, if you are considering a career in the field of software development and are looking for a good language to become proficient in, Rust is an excellent choice. Because of its widespread adoption and use in a wide variety of technological organisations, it is an excellent language to have on your resume. If you are applying for a job in the field of information technology, this is especially important.

The computer programming language known as Rust places a significant focus not only on performance but also on concurrency. It places a significant amount of emphasis on preventing common programming errors such as null or dangling pointer references, both of which can lead to segmentation faults and other problems. It does this by placing a significant amount of emphasis on preventing common programming errors. Because Rust is a statically typed programming language, the type of a variable must be determined before the programme can be compiled. This is a prerequisite for the process. This leads to code that is safer and more predictable, and it can be helpful in catching bugs early on in the development process.

The programming language known as Rust places a significant emphasis on being able to write programmes that run in parallel. This indicates that the language was designed with the goal of simplifying the process of creating programmes that can run in parallel with other applications. Because of this, writing high-performance programmes that take advantage of multi-core processors might be an area in which Rust shines as a viable alternative. The community that lies in and around Rust is a thriving one that is still growing. It is an encouraging environment for programmers of varying levels of experience because the Rust community places a high value on things like empathy, inclusivity, and constructive behaviour. Rust is currently being utilised in a wide variety of fields, including web development, systems programming, game development, and machine learning, to name just a few of these fields' applications. Because of this, having knowledge of Rust can open up a large number of doors for you in terms of potential careers to pursue.

Rust Over Other Programming Languages?

Rust is superior to many other programming languages in a number of respects, including the following:

1. Rust places a strong emphasis on safety, with one of its primary goals being the elimination of common programming errors such as null or dangling pointer references, both of which can lead to segmentation faults and other problems. It accomplishes this by utilizing a combination of a borrowing and ownership system as well as a type system that assists in the early detection of bugs during the process of software development.

2. The programming language Rust places a significant emphasis on concurrent programming, which makes it simple to compose programmes that can be executed in parallel with one another. It supports concurrent programming and comes with a number of built-in features, such as atomic reference counting and support for message passing, among other features.

3. Rust is a statically-typed language with a fast compiler, which means it can produce efficient code that runs at a speed that is comparable to that of C and C++. Rust's performance is characterized by its ability to produce code with these characteristics. It also has a number of features that make it simple to write code that has a high performance level, such as the ability to manually manage memory and control low-level details of how code is executed. Both of these capabilities make it easier to write code that has a high performance level.

4. Productivity: Despite the fact that its primary concerns are safety and performance, the Rust programming language is intended to be a productive one to use. It has a syntax that is uncomplicated and easy to understand, a powerful macro system, and a number of built-in tools that can assist with testing and debugging programmes.

5. Community: The Rust programming language has an active and helpful community of software developers who are committed to advancing the language and facilitating the education of others. Because the Rust community places a high value on empathy, inclusiveness, and constructive behavior, it is an encouraging environment for programmers of varying degrees of experience.

Rust Over Python

Rust and Python are both powerful programming languages; however, each was designed for a different application scenario and offers its users a different and distinct collection of benefits.

Rust is a statically-typed programming language that was developed with the objectives of maximising concurrency, performance, and safety. Rust is a language that is used to write computer programmes. It places a significant emphasis on avoiding typical programming errors and is ideally suited for activities that call for a high level of control over the underlying hardware. Some examples of activities that call for this level of control include the development of computer games and computer systems.

Python, on the other hand, is a dynamically typed programming language that is well-known for its user-friendliness, readability, and adaptability. Python is a dynamic programming language. Data analysis, the development of websites, and scientific computing are three examples of common applications for the tool. All of these applications frequently require rapid prototyping or scripting, which is why the tool was created.

Python is a good choice for tasks that generally require a high level of productivity and ease of use, and Rust is a good choice for tasks that generally require a high level of performance and safety. Python is a good choice for tasks that generally require a high level of productivity and ease of use. In the end, the specific requirements and goals of the project that you are working on will determine which language you should use to communicate with others about the project.

Rust Over C++ and Go

It is essential to keep in mind that programming languages are merely tools, and that selecting which tool to use is determined by the particular requirements and objectives of a project. It is not accurate to say that C++ is "weak against" Rust or that Go is "not as good as" Rust because there is no language that is objectively "better" than every other language in every circumstance.

In light of this, the following are some of the ways in which Rust and Go are distinct from C++ and from one another:

C++:
C++ is a compiled language that uses statically typed data. Because of this, the types of variables have to be specified during the compilation process, and the programme has to be converted into machine code before it can be executed. C++ is a very low-level programming language, which gives it a great deal of control and flexibility but also makes it more difficult to write and debug programmes written in C++. If it is not used carefully, C++ can have a reputation for being quick, but it also has a risk of memory errors and security vulnerabilities.

Rust:
Rust is a programming language that, like C++, is statically typed and compiled, but it places a significant emphasis on concurrency and safety. Borrow checker is a feature of the Rust programming language that helps prevent common types of memory errors, such as null or dangling pointer references. Rust also features a robust macro system and provides support for high-level abstractions, both of which contribute to the language's ability to simplify the process of writing and maintaining large codebases.

Go:
Go is a programming language that is statically typed and compiled, with an emphasis on concurrency, simplicity, and performance. There is a garbage collector in Go, which can be useful for memory management, but it also has the potential to add overhead and make the programme less predictable. Because Go has an inbuilt concurrency model that is based on "goroutines" and channels, it is possible to write parallel code more quickly using this programming language.

In a nutshell, C++, Rust, and Go are all highly effective programming languages, each of which has its own set of advantages and drawbacks. C++ is a low-level programming language that offers a great deal of control and flexibility, but it can be more challenging to write code in and troubleshoot. Rust is a statically-typed programming language that places a significant emphasis on both concurrency and safety. The programming language Go is statically typed and places an emphasis on concurrency, performance, and ease of use. The particular requirements and objectives of a project should guide the decision of which method to implement.

Basics of Rust Syntax

Some basic syntax elements you should know when programming in Rust:

1. Variables: Variables in Rust are defined using the let keyword, followed by the variable name and the type. Let's take a look at the following example:

```
let x: i32 = 5;
let y: f64 = 3.14;
let name: &str = "John";
```

2. Functions: Functions in Rust are defined using the fn keyword, followed by the function name, the arguments, and the return type. Let's take a look at the following example:

```
fn add(x: i32, y: i32) -> i32 {
    x + y
}
```

3. Control flow: Rust has the usual control flow statements such as if and loop, as well as the match statement, which is similar to a switch statement in other languages. Let's take a look at the following example:

```
let x = 5;

if x > 0 {
    println!("x is positive");
} else {
    println!("x is negative or zero");
}

loop {
    println!("This loop will run forever");
}
```

```rust
let y = 5;

match y {
    1 => println!("y is 1"),
    2 => println!("y is 2"),
    _ => println!("y is something else"),
}
```

4. Structs: Structs in Rust are used to define custom data types. They can have any number of fields, each with its own type. Let's take a look at the following example:

```rust
struct Point {
    x: i32,
    y: i32,
}

let p = Point { x: 5, y: 10 };
```

5. Traits: Traits in Rust are used to define shared behavior among types. They can have methods and associated types, and are similar to interfaces in other languages. Let's take a look at the following example:

```rust
trait Animal {
    fn make_sound(&self) ->&'static str;
}

struct Dog;

impl Animal for Dog {
    fn make_sound(&self) ->&'static str {
        "bark"
    }
}

let dog = Dog;
println!("The dog says {}", dog.make_sound());
```

Program 'Hello world'

Before you begin to write applications in Rust, it is important that you have a solid understanding of the following core concepts:

Rust is a statically typed programming language, which implies that when you construct variables and function arguments, you are required to specify the types of those variables and arguments. Take, for instance:

```rust
let x: i32 = 5;
let y: f64 = 3.14;

fn add(a: i32, b: i32) -> i32 {
    a + b
}
```

Rust places a significant emphasis on ownership and borrowing as a means of controlling the variables and data over the course of their lifetimes. Every value in Rust has an owner, and when that owner leaves the scope of the value's application, the value is deleted automatically (freed from memory).

The macro system in Rust is quite robust, and it gives you the ability to build your own unique syntax for your code. The macro rules! syntax is used to define macros, and the #[...] notation is used to invoke them when they are needed.

Integers, floating-point numbers, booleans, and characters are some of the built-in data types that are available in the Rust programming language. In addition to that, it provides support for arrays, tuples, and a great deal of additional types.

If you can keep these fundamental ideas straight in your head, you should be able to construct a rudimentary "hello, world" application in Rust:

```rust
fn main() {
    println!("Hello, world!");
}
```

This programme may be executed by using the cargo run command, which will both construct and execute your code.

My First Program: Creating a Calculator

Now that we have covered the fundamentals of Rust programming, it is time to put those skills to use by developing a basic application. In this lesson, you will learn how to construct a calculator application using only a few lines of code.

To create a simple calculator program in Rust, you can follow these steps:

1. Start by creating a new Rust project using cargo:

```
cargo new calculator
```

2. This will create a new directory called calculator, with the following file structure:

```
calculator
├── Cargo.toml
└── src
    └──
```

3. Open in your favorite text editor and add the following code:

```rust
use std::io;

fn main() {
    println!("Welcome to the calculator!");

    loop {
        println!("Enter an expression to calculate (e.g. 2 + 2):");

        let mut input = String::new();
        io::stdin().read_line(&mut input).expect("Failed to read input");
        let input = input.trim();
```

```rust
        if input == "exit" {
            println!("Goodbye!");
            break;
        }

        let result = calculate(input);
        println!("Result: {}", result);
    }
}

fn calculate(input: &str) -> f64 {
    // TODO: Implement the calculation
    0.0
}
```

This code creates a simple command-line interface that allows the user to enter an expression to calculate, and will print the result. The calculate function is where you will implement the actual calculation.

4. To implement the calculation, you will need to parse the input string to extract the numbers and the operator. There are many ways to do this, but one simple way is to use a regular expression to match the pattern of a number, followed by an operator, followed by another number.

The following is an illustration of how you can use a regular expression to parse the input string in order to retrieve the numerical values and operators:

```rust
use regex::Regex;

fn calculate(input: &str) -> f64 {
    let re = Regex::new(r"([\d.]+)\s*([+-/*])\s*([\d.]+)").unwrap();
    let captures = re.captures(input).unwrap();

    let num1: f64 = captures[1].parse().unwrap();
    let num2: f64 = captures[3].parse().unwrap();
    let op = &captures[2];
```

```rust
    // TODO: Perform the calculation
    0.0
}
```

5. Now that you have extracted the numbers and operator from the input string, you can
perform the calculation. You can use a simple match statement to determine which
operator was used and perform the appropriate calculation:

```rust
fn calculate(input: &str) -> f64 {
    let         re         =         Regex::new(r"([\d.]+)\s*([+-
/*])\s*([\d.]+)").unwrap();
    let captures = re.captures(input).unwrap();

    let num1: f64 = captures[1].parse().unwrap();
    let num2: f64 = captures[3].parse().unwrap();
    let op = &captures[2];

    match op {
        "+" => num1 + num2,
        "-" => num1 - num2,
        "*" => num
```

6. You can then complete the calculate function by handling the remaining operators:

```rust
fn calculate(input: &str) -> f64 {
    let         re         =         Regex::new(r"([\d.]+)\s*([+-
/*])\s*([\d.]+)").unwrap();
    let captures = re.captures(input).unwrap();

    let num1: f64 = captures[1].parse().unwrap();
    let num2: f64 = captures[3].parse().unwrap();
    let op = &captures[2];

    match op {
        "+" => num1 + num2,
        "-" => num1 - num2,
        "*" => num1 * num2,
```

```
            "/" => num1 / num2,
            _ => panic!("Invalid operator"),
        }
    }
}
```

Now that you have implemented the calculate function, you can test your calculator by running the program with cargo run. You should be able to enter an expression to calculate, and the program will print the result.

```
Welcome to the calculator!
Enter an expression to calculate (e.g. 2 + 2):
2 + 2
Result: 4
Enter an expression to calculate (e.g. 2 + 2):
2 * 3
Result: 6
Enter an expression to calculate (e.g. 2 + 2):
exit
Goodbye!
```

CHAPTER 2: GETTING READY WITH RUST ENVIRONMENT

Setting Up Rust on Windows

To set up a Rust development environment on Windows, you can follow these steps:

- Download and install the Rust programming language by visiting the official Rust website at https://www.rust-lang.org/ and clicking the "Download" button. This will download and install the latest version of Rust, along with the cargo package manager.

- Once the installation is complete, open a command prompt and verify that Rust is installed by running the following command:

```
rustc --version
```

- This will print the version of Rust that you have installed.

- Next, you will need a text editor or Integrated Development Environment (IDE) to write your Rust code. Some popular options include Visual Studio Code, Eclipse, and CLion. You can use any text editor that you prefer, as long as it has support for Rust syntax highlighting.

- Once you have a text editor set up, you can create a new Rust project using cargo:

```
cargo new myproject
```

This will create a new directory called myproject with the following file structure:

```
myproject
├── Cargo.toml
└── src
    └──
```

1. You can then open the file in your text editor and start writing Rust code. to build and run your code, you can use the cargo run command from the command prompt:

```
cd myproject
cargo run
```

This will build and run your code, and will print the output to the command prompt.When the Rust installer is finished, you'll be ready to program with Rust. You won't have a convenient IDE yet. and you're not yet set up to call Windows APIs. But you could launch a command prompt (cmd.exe), and perhaps issue the command cargo --version. If you see a version number printed, then that confirms that Rust installed correctly.

Since you have successfully installed the Rust development environment on your Windows computer, you are free to begin educating yourself about the Rust programming language and creating your very own software applications.

Here are a few things you might want to do next:

- Write some simple programs to practice your Rust skills. You might start with a "hello, world" program, and then move on to more complex programs like a calculator as you learned in chapter 1.

- Learn about Rust's ownership and borrowing system, which is a key feature of the language that allows you to manage the lifetime of your variables and data.

- Experiment with Rust's macro system, which allows you to define custom syntax for your code.

- Join the Rust community and get involved in online forums, IRC channels, and other resources. You can find a list of community resources at https://www.rust-lang.org/community.

Setting Up Rust on Linux

To set up Rust on Linux, you will need to have a compatible version of the Linux operating system and a compatible version of the Rust compiler.

1. First, ensure that your Linux system is up to date by running the following command:

```
sudo apt update
sudo apt upgrade
```

2. Next, install the necessary dependencies for building Rust. This can be done using the following command:

```
sudo apt install build-essential
```

3. Next, you will need to install the Rust compiler. The recommended way to install Rust is through the Rustup tool, which is a command-line utility that manages Rust versions and enables you to switch between them. to install Rustup, run the following command:

```
curl --proto '=https' --tlsv1.2 -sSf
https://sh.rustup.rs | sh
```

4. This will download and run the Rustup installation script, which will prompt you to choose an installation option. to install the stable version of Rust, press 1 and then press Enter.

5. The Rustup tool will now install the Rust compiler and its dependencies. This may take a few minutes.

6. Once the installation is complete, you can verify that the Rust compiler is working by running the following command:

```
rustc --version
```

7. Finally, you may want to add the Rust installation directory to your system's PATH environment variable, so that you can use the Rust compiler and other Rust tools from any directory. to do this, add the following line to your .bashrc or .bash_profile file:

```
export PATH="$HOME/.cargo/bin:$PATH"
```

8. Save the file and then run the following command to apply the changes:

```
source ~/.bashrc
```

With these steps, you should now have Rust installed and configured on your Linux system.

Installing Crates and Cargo on Windows

To install crates (libraries) in the Rust programming language on Windows, you will need to have the Rust compiler and package manager installed on your system.

1. First, ensure that you have the Rust compiler installed by running the following command:

```
rustc --version
```

2. Download the Rust compiler: You can download the Rust compiler from the official website at https://www.rust-lang.org/. Click on the "Download" button and select the "Windows" option from the dropdown menu. This will download the Rust installer.

3. Run the Rust installer: Double-click on the downloaded installer file and follow the on-screen instructions to install Rust. Make sure to accept the license agreement and select the destination folder for the installation.

4. Set up the Rust environment: After the installation is complete, you will need to set up the Rust environment. Open the Command Prompt and type the following command:

```
rustup default stable
```

This will set the default Rust toolchain to the stable version. You can also use other toolchains, such as the beta or nightly versions, by specifying them with the rustup default command.

5. Next, you will need to install the Rust package manager, Cargo. Cargo is included with the Rust compiler, so if you have already installed Rust, you should already have Cargo installed. You can check if Cargo is installed by running the following command:

```
cargo --version
```

6. With the Rust compiler and Cargo installed, you can use Cargo to install crates (libraries) for your Rust projects. to install a crate, navigate to the root directory of your Rust project and run the following command:

```
cargo install crate_name
```

Replace "crate_name" with the name of the crate you want to install. For example, to install the "serde" crate, you would run the following command:

```
cargo install serde
```

Cargo will download and build the crate, and then add it to your project's dependencies. You can then use the crate in your Rust code by including the following line at the top of your Rust file:

```
extern crate crate_name;
```

Replace "crate_name" with the name of the crate you installed.

Installing Crates and Cargo on Linux

To install crates (libraries) and Cargo (the Rust package manager) on a Linux machine, you will need to follow these steps:

1. Set up the Rust environment: After the installation is complete, you will need to set up the Rust environment. Open a terminal and type the following command:

```
rustup default stable
```

This will set the default Rust toolchain to the stable version. You can also use other toolchains, such as the beta or nightly versions, by specifying them with the rustup default command.

2. Install a crate: to install a crate, you can use the cargo install command. For example, to install the clap crate, which provides a command-line argument parser, you can use the following command:

```
cargo install clap
```

This will download and install the clap crate, as well as any dependencies it may have. You can also specify a specific version of the crate by adding the --version flag, like so:

```
cargo install clap --version 2.33.0
```

Use a crate in your project: to use a crate in your Rust project, you will need to add it to your Cargo.toml file. Open the Cargo.toml file in your project and add the following line to the [dependencies] section:

```
clap = "2.33.0"
```

This will tell Cargo to include the clap crate as a dependency when building your project. You can then use the crate in your Rust code by adding the following line to the top of your file:

```
use clap::{App, Arg};
```

That's it! You have successfully installed crates and Cargo on your Linux machine. You can now use Cargo to manage the dependencies of your Rust projects and use crates to add functionality to your programs.

Installing Visual Studio Code on Window

You will need to follow these steps in order to successfully instal Visual Studio Code (VS Code) on a Windows PC in order to develop with Rust:

1. Download Visual Studio Code: You can download Visual Studio Code from the official website at https://code.visualstudio.com/. Click on the "Download" button and follow the on-screen instructions to download and run the VS Code installer.
2. Install the Rust extension: After installing VS Code, you will need to install the Rust extension. to do this, follow these steps:
3. Open VS Code and click on the "Extensions" icon in the left sidebar.
4. Type "Rust" in the search bar and press Enter.
5. Select the "Rust (rls)" extension from the list of results and click on the "Install" button.

6. This will install the Rust extension, which provides support for Rust development in VS Code.
7. Configure the Rust extension: After installing the Rust extension, you will need to configure it to use the Rust compiler and Cargo package manager. to do this, follow these steps:
8. Open the Command Prompt and type the following command:

```
rustup show
```

9. This will display the path to the Rust compiler and Cargo package manager on your system.
10. Copy the path to the Rust compiler and Cargo package manager.
11. Open VS Code and click on the "File" menu, then select "Preferences" and "Settings".
12. In the search bar, type "Rust" and press Enter.
13. In the "Rust: RLS" section, paste the path to the Rust compiler and Cargo package manager in the "Path to Rustc" and "Path to Cargo" fields, respectively.

14. This will configure the Rust extension to use the Rust compiler and Cargo package manager on your system.

15. Test the installation: to test the installation, create a new Rust project in VS Code. to do this, follow these steps:
16. Click on the "File" menu and select "New Folder".
17. Type a name for the folder and press Enter.
18. Right-click on the folder and select "Open with Code".
19. In the terminal, navigate to the folder and type the following command:

```
cargo init
```

This will create a new Rust project in the folder. You should see the Rust extension automatically detect the project and provide features such as code completion, formatting, and linting.

That's it! You have successfully installed Visual Studio Code on your Windows machine for Rust development. You can now use VS Code to write and debug Rust programs.

Installing Visual Studio Code on Linux

To install Visual Studio Code (VS Code) on a Linux machine for Rust development, you will need to follow these steps:

1. Download Visual Studio Code: You can download Visual Studio Code from the official website at https://code.visualstudio.com/. Click on the "Download" button and select the "Linux" option from the dropdown menu. This will download the VS Code installation package for Linux.

2. Install Visual Studio Code: to install VS Code on Linux, you will need to extract the installation package and run the installer. to do this, follow these steps:
   - Open a terminal and navigate to the directory where you downloaded the VS Code installation package.
   - Extract the installation package by typing the following command:

```
tar -xvf code_*.tar.gz
```

   - This will extract the files from the installation package into a new directory.
   - Navigate to the new directory and run the VS Code installer by typing the following command:

```
./code
```

This will launch the VS Code installer. Follow the on-screen instructions to complete the installation.

3. Install the Rust extension: After installing VS Code, you will need to install the Rust extension. to do this, follow these steps:
   - Open VS Code and click on the "Extensions" icon in the left sidebar.
   - Type "Rust" in the search bar and press Enter.
   - Select the "Rust (rls)" extension from the list of results and click on the "Install" button.
   - This will install the Rust extension, which provides support for Rust development in VS Code.

4. Configure the Rust extension: After installing the Rust extension, you will need to configure it to use the Rust compiler and Cargo package manager. to do this, follow these steps:
*   Open a terminal and type the following command:

```
rustup show
```

*   This will display the path to the Rust compiler and Cargo package manager on your system.
*   Copy the path to the Rust compiler and Cargo package manager.
*   Open VS Code and click on the "File" menu, then select "Preferences" and "Settings".
*   In the search bar, type "Rust" and press Enter.
*   In the "Rust: RLS" section, paste the path to the Rust compiler and Cargo package manager in the "Path to Rustc" and "Path to Cargo" fields, respectively.

This will configure the Rust extension to use the Rust compiler and Cargo package manager on your system.

5. Test the installation: to test the installation, create a new Rust project in VS Code. to do this, follow these steps:
    *   Click on the "File" menu and select "New Folder".
    *   Type a name for the folder and press Enter.
    *   Right-click on the folder and select "Open with Code".
    *   In the terminal, navigate to the folder and type the following command:

```
cargo init
```

This will create a new Rust project in the folder. You should see the Rust extension automatically detect the project and provide features such as code completion, formatting, and linting.

Chapter 3: Most Essentials of Rust

Variables

A term that points to a value that is kept in memory is referred to as a variable in the Rust programming language. The default behaviour of variables in Rust is for them to be immutable; this means that once a value is bound to a variable, it cannot be altered in any way. You have to make use of the mut keyword in order to construct a mutable variable.

Following is an example of declaring and assigning a value to an immutable variable:

```
let x = 5;
```

Following is an example of declaring and assigning a value to a mutable variable:

```
let mut y = 10;
```

You can also declare a variable and assign a value to it later, like this:

```
let z;
z = 15;
```

It's important to note that when declaring a variable and assigning a value to it later, you must use the mut keyword if you want the variable to be mutable.

You can also declare a variable and assign it a type, like this:

```
let a: i32 = 20;
```

This creates an i32 variable called a and assigns it the value 20.You can also specify the type of a mutable variable when declaring it:

```
let mut b: f64 = 3.14;
```

This creates a mutable f64 variable called b and assigns it the value 3.14.

It's generally a good idea to specify the type of a variable when declaring it, as it helps the Rust compiler catch type-related errors at compile time.

Now, lets look at some advanced aspects of variables in Rust, namely shadowing. In shadowing, Rust allows you to "shadow" a variable, which means declaring a new variable with the same name as an existing variable. When you shadow a variable, the new variable has the same value as the original, but you can change the value of the new variable and it won't affect the original. Shadowing is often used to change the type of a variable, like this:

```rust
let x = 5;
let x: f64 = x as f64;
```

In the given example, the original x is an i32 with the value 5, and the new x is a f64 with the same value. Shadowing can also be used to change the mutability of a variable:

```rust
let mut x = 5;
let x = x; // x is now immutable
```

Lets try another way or an example to understand what shadowing of a variable is. For example, if a programmer has a variable called "x" which is set to the value 10 and they want to temporarily change the value to 5, they could use shadowing to do this. The code would look something like this:

```rust
let x = 10;
let x = 5;
```

This code uses shadowing to overwrite the value of "x" to 5 while still retaining the original value of 10. After the code is finished running, "x" will still have the value of 10. Shadowing is a great way to temporarily change the value of a variable without losing the original value.

Constants

A constant is a value that is fixed at compile-time and cannot be changed at runtime. Constants are often used to represent values that are used frequently in a program and do not need to be modified, such as mathematical constants or physical constants.

To define a constant in Rust, you can use the const keyword, like this:

```rust
const MAX_POINTS: u32 = 100_000;
```

In the given example, MAX_POINTS is a constant with the type u32 (unsigned 32-bit integer) and a value of 100_000. The type of a constant must be annotated, and the value must be a compile-time constant expression, which means it can be calculated by the compiler at compile-time.

Constants have a number of restrictions in Rust. For example, they must be annotated with their type, they must be defined in the global scope, outside of any function, and they cannot be mutable.

Let's take a look at another example of a constant in Rust:

```rust
const GRAVITATIONAL_CONSTANT: f64 = 6.674e-11;
```

In the given example, GRAVITATIONAL_CONSTANT is a constant with the type f64 (64-bit floating point number) and a value of 6.674e-11. This constant represents the gravitational constant in physics, which is a fundamental physical constant that is used to calculate the gravitational force between two objects.

Let me give you some more examples of constants and how they work:

```rust
const PI: f64 = 3.14159265358979323384626433;

const AVG_MONTHLY_RAINFALL: f32 = 3.0;

const US_POPULATION: u64 = 331_000_000;

const MAX_SPEED: u8 = 255;

const MAX_TEMPERATURE: i8 = 100;
```

In these examples:

PI is a constant with the type f64 (64-bit floating point number) and a value of approximately 3.14.
AVG_MONTHLY_RAINFALL is a constant with the type f32 (32-bit floating point number) and a value of 3.0.

US_POPULATION is a constant with the type u64 (unsigned 64-bit integer) and a value of 331,000,000.

MAX_SPEED is a constant with the type u8 (unsigned 8-bit integer) and a value of 255.

MAX_TEMPERATURE is a constant with the type i8 (signed 8-bit integer) and a value of 100.

Constants Vs Immutable Variables

There is a distinction made in Rust between variables that cannot be changed and those that are constant.

Constants are values that are fixed at compile-time and cannot be changed at runtime. They are defined using the const keyword and must be annotated with their type. Constants have a number of restrictions, such as being defined in the global scope, outside of any function, and not being mutable.

On the other hand, immutable variables are variables that cannot be modified after they have been initialized. They are defined using the let keyword and do not need to be annotated with their type, because the Rust compiler can infer the type from the value being assigned. Immutable variables can be defined in any scope, including inside functions, and they can be shadowed (re-assigned) by another let binding with the same name in a different scope.

Following is an example that illustrates the difference between constants and immutable variables:

```rust
fn main() {
    // This is a constant defined with the `const`
keyword.
    // It must be annotated with its type and is
defined in the global scope.
```

```rust
    const MAX_POINTS: u32 = 100_000;

    // This is an immutable variable defined with the
`let` keyword.
    // It does not need to be annotated with its type,
because the Rust compiler can infer it from the value
being assigned.
    // It is defined inside a function, so it is not in
the global scope.
    let current_points = 50_000;

    // The value of an immutable variable can be read,
but it cannot be modified.
    // This line of code would produce an error,
because current_points is an immutable variable.
    // current_points = 75_000;

    // However, it is possible to shadow an immutable
variable with a new `let` binding with the same name.
    // This creates a new variable that shadows the old
one, effectively "re-assigning" the value.
    let current_points = 75_000;

    // The value of a constant can also be read, but it
cannot be modified.
    // This line of code would produce an error,
because MAX_POINTS is a constant.
    // MAX_POINTS = 75_000;
}
```

Necessity of Constant Against Variables

Constants and immutable variables serve different purposes.

Constants are values that are fixed at compile-time and cannot be changed at runtime. They are defined using the const keyword and must be annotated with their type. Constants are often used to represent values that are used frequently in a program and do not need to be modified, such as mathematical constants or physical constants.

On the other hand, immutable variables are variables that cannot be modified after they have been initialized. They are defined using the let keyword and do not need to be annotated with their type, because the Rust compiler can infer the type from the value being assigned. Immutable variables can be defined in any scope, including inside functions, and they can be shadowed (re-assigned) by another let binding with the same name in a different scope.

Following is an example that illustrates the difference between constants and immutable variables:

```
fn main() {
    // This is a constant defined with the `const`
keyword.
    // It must be annotated with its type and is
defined in the global scope.
    const PI: f64 =
3.141592653589793238462643383279502884197169399375510;

    // This is an immutable variable defined with the
`let` keyword.
    // It does not need to be annotated with its type,
because the Rust compiler can infer it from the value
being assigned.
    // It is defined inside a function, so it is not in
the global scope.
    let radius = 2.0;

    // The value of PI cannot be modified, because it
is a constant.
    // This line of code would produce an error,
because PI is a constant.
    // PI = 3.14;

    // The value of radius can be read, but it cannot
be modified.
```

```rust
    // This line of code would produce an error,
because radius is an immutable variable.
    // radius = 2.5;

    // However, it is possible to shadow the immutable
variable radius with a new `let` binding with the same
name.
    // This creates a new variable that shadows the old
one, effectively "re-assigning" the value.
    let radius = 2.5;
}
```

In the given example, PI is a constant with the type f64 (64-bit floating point number) and a value of approximately 3.14. It represents the mathematical constant pi, which is used to calculate the circumference and area of a circle. radius is an immutable variable with the type f64 (64-bit floating point number) and an initial value of 2.0. It represents the radius of a circle.

As you can see, constants and immutable variables serve different purposes in Rust. Constants are used to represent values that do not need to be modified, while immutable variables are used to represent values that may change within a certain scope, but cannot be modified after they have been initialized.

Shadowing Vs Mutability

Shadowing is a way to "re-assign" the value of a variable by creating a new variable with the same name that shadows the old one. Shadowing is often used when you want to change the value of a variable within a certain scope, but you do not want to modify the value of the original variable.

On the other hand, mutability allows you to modify the value of a variable directly, without creating a new variable. Mutability is often used when you want to update the value of a variable multiple times throughout your code.

Following is an example that illustrates the difference between shadowing and mutability in Rust:

```rust
fn main() {
    // This is an immutable variable defined with the
`let` keyword.
    let x = 5;

    // This is a mutable variable defined with the
`let` keyword and the `mut` keyword.
    let mut y = 5;

    // The value of an immutable variable cannot be
modified.
    // This line of code would produce an error,
because x is an immutable variable.
    // x = 10;

    // However, it is possible to shadow the immutable
variable x with a new `let` binding with the same name.
    // This creates a new variable that shadows the old
one, effectively "re-assigning" the value.
    let x = 10;

    // The value of a mutable variable can be modified
directly.
    y = 10;

    println!("x = {}", x); // prints "x = 10"
    println!("y = {}", y); // prints "y = 10"
}
```

In the given example, x is an immutable variable with an initial value of 5. It is shadowed by a new let binding with the same name that assigns a new value of 10. y is a mutable variable with an initial value of 5. Its value is directly modified to 10.

As you can see, shadowing allows you to change the value of a variable within a certain scope, but it does not modify the original variable. Mutability allows you to directly modify the value of a variable, but it requires the use of the mut keyword.

You should choose between shadowing and mutability depending on the specific behavior you want your code to have. If you want to change the value of a variable within a certain scope, but you do not want to modify the original variable, you can use shadowing. If you want to directly modify the value of a variable, you can use mutability.

Functions

In Rust, a function is a block of code that performs a specific task and may or may not return a value. Functions are a fundamental building block of Rust programs and are used to encapsulate code that can be called multiple times from different parts of a program.

Following is an example of a simple Rust function that takes two integers as input and returns their sum:

```rust
fn add(x: i32, y: i32) -> i32 {
    x + y
}
```

This function, called add, takes two arguments, x and y, which are both i32 (32-bit signed integer) values. The function also has a return type of i32, indicated by the -> i32 syntax. The function body consists of a single line of code that adds x and y together and returns the result.

To call this function from elsewhere in your program, you would use the following syntax:

```rust
let sum = add(5, 10);
```

This would assign the value 15 to the variable sum, since 5 + 10 = 15.

Functions in Rust can also have more complex types for their arguments and return values, and they can have multiple statements in their bodies. For example, here is a function that takes a vector of strings and returns the longest string in the vector:

```rust
fn longest_string(strings: Vec<String>) -> String {
    let mut longest = strings[0].clone();
    for s in strings {
```

```rust
        if s.len() > longest.len() {
            longest = s;
        }
    }
    longest
}
```

This function takes a vector of strings as its argument and returns a string. It uses a mutable variable longest to keep track of the longest string seen so far, and it iterates through the input vector to find the longest string. Finally, it returns the longest string.

Types of Functions In Rust

There are several types of functions that can be defined, each with its own characteristics and use cases. Here are some of the most common types of functions in Rust:

- Free functions: These are standalone functions that are not associated with any particular struct or object. They are defined using the fn keyword, and they can be called from anywhere in the program.

- Method functions: These are functions that are associated with a struct or an object, and they can be called using the . operator. Method functions are defined using the fn keyword, but they are preceded by the impl keyword and have a special syntax for their first argument, called the self argument.

- Closure functions: These are anonymous functions that can capture variables from the surrounding scope and can be stored in a variable or passed as an argument to another function. Closure functions are defined using the | syntax, and they can be called using the () operator.

- Generator functions: These are functions that can be used to generate an iterator, which can be used to yield a sequence of values. Generator functions are defined using the yield keyword and the move keyword, and they can be called using the .next() method.

Following is an example that illustrates some of these types of functions in action:

```rust
fn main() {
```

```rust
    // Free function
    println!("The sum of 3 and 4 is {}", add(3, 4));

    // Method function
    let point = Point { x: 5, y: 10 };
    println!("The distance from the origin is {}",
point.distance_from_origin());

    // Closure function
    let add_two = |x| x + 2;
    println!("3 plus 2 is {}", add_two(3));

    // Generator function
    let mut generator = count_up_from(5);
    println!("{}", generator.next().unwrap());
    println!("{}", generator.next().unwrap());
}

// Free function
fn add(x: i32, y: i32) -> i32 {
    x + y
}

// Method function
struct Point {
    x: i32,
    y: i32,
}

impl Point {
    fn distance_from_origin(&self) -> f64 {
        (self.x.pow(2) + self.y.pow(2)).sqrt()
    }
}

// Closure function
let add_two = |x| x + 2;
```

```rust
// Generator function
fn count_up_from(start: i32) -> impl Iterator<Item=i32>
{
    (start..).into_iter()
}
```

Writing a Rust Function

Writing your first function in Rust is easy! Here is a simple example of a Rust function that takes an integer as input and returns the square of that integer:

```rust
fn square(x: i32) -> i32 {
    x * x
}
```

To call this function from elsewhere in your program, you would use the following syntax:

```rust
let y = square(5);
```

This would assign the value 25 to the variable y, since 5 * 5 = 25.

Here is a complete example program that shows how to define and call this function:

```rust
fn main() {
    let x = 5;
    let y = square(x);
    println!("The square of {} is {}", x, y);
}

fn square(x: i32) -> i32 {
    x * x
}
```

This program would output the following line to the console:

Coding a Function with an Iterator

Writing a Rust function that uses an iterator can be a bit more involved than writing a simple function, as it requires understanding the concept of iterators and how to work with them. However, once you understand the basic principles, writing functions with iterators is not necessarily difficult.

An iterator is an object that represents a sequence of values that can be iterated over. In Rust, iterators are implemented using the Iterator trait, which defines a set of methods that must be implemented in order to create a custom iterator.

Following is an example of a Rust function that takes an iterator of integers as input and returns the sum of all the elements in the iterator:

```rust
fn sum_iterator(iter: impl Iterator<Item=i32>) -> i32 {
    let mut sum = 0;
    for x in iter {
        sum += x;
    }
    sum
}
```

This function takes an iterator of i32 values as its input and returns an i32 value. It uses a mutable variable sum to keep track of the sum so far, and it iterates over the input iterator using a for loop. For each element x in the iterator, it adds x to the sum and then moves on to the next element. Finally, it returns the sum.

To call this function from elsewhere in your program, you would use the following syntax:

```rust
let v = vec![1, 2, 3, 4];
let s = sum_iterator(v.into_iter());
```

This would assign the value 10 to the variable s, since $1 + 2 + 3 + 4 = 10$.

Passing Function As Arguments

Passing a function as an argument to another function is useful when you want to reuse a common piece of code in multiple places, or when you want to abstract over the behavior of a function.

To pass a function as an argument, you need to specify the function's signature as the type of the argument. The function signature consists of the function's name, its argument types, and its return type.

Following is an example of a Rust function that takes another function as an argument:

```
fn apply_twice<F>(f: F, x: i32) -> i32
    where F: Fn(i32) -> i32
{
    f(f(x))
}
```

This function, called apply_twice, takes a function f as its first argument and an integer x as its second argument. It has a generic type parameter F, which represents the type of the function f. The type parameter is constrained by the trait Fn, which means that f must be a function that takes an i32 value as its input and returns an i32 value.

The function body consists of a single line of code that calls the function f twice on the input x and returns the result.

To call this function from elsewhere in your program, you would use the following syntax:

```
let double = |x| x * 2;
let y = apply_twice(double, 5);
```

This would assign the value 20 to the variable y, since (5 * 2) * 2 = 20.

Nested Function (Function Within Function)

A function within a function, also known as a nested function, is a function that is defined inside another function. Nested functions can be useful when you want to define a function that is only used within a specific context, or when you want to break down a larger function into smaller, more manageable pieces.

To define a nested function in Rust, you simply define the function inside the body of another function using the fn keyword. The nested function has access to the variables and arguments of the outer function, and it can be called from within the outer function just like any other function.

Following is an example of a Rust function that contains a nested function:

```rust
fn outer(x: i32) -> i32 {
    fn inner(y: i32) -> i32 {
        x + y
    }

    inner(5)
}
```

This function, called outer, takes an integer x as its argument and defines a nested function called inner that takes an integer y as its argument and returns the sum of x and y. The body of the outer function calls the inner function with the argument 5 and returns the result.

To call the outer function from elsewhere in your program, you would use the following syntax:

```rust
let z = outer(3);
```

This would assign the value 8 to the variable z, since 3 + 5 = 8.

Check out another detailed example of a Rust function that contains a nested function:

```rust
fn outer(x: i32) -> i32 {
```

```rust
    // Nested function
    fn inner(y: i32) -> i32 {
        x + y
    }

    // Use the nested function
    let result = inner(5);

    // Return the result
    result
}

fn main() {
    let a = 3;
    let b = outer(a);
    println!("The result is {}", b);
}
```

This program defines a function outer that takes an integer x as its argument and returns an integer. The outer function contains a nested function called inner that takes an integer y as its argument and returns the sum of x and y.

The outer function calls the inner function with the argument 5 and stores the result in the variable result. It then returns the result as its own return value.

In the main function, the program calls the outer function with the argument 3 and prints the result to the console. The output of the program is:

```
The result is 8
```

Built-In Functions

Rust has a large number of built-in functions that are available for use in your programs. These functions are provided by the standard library and cover a wide range of tasks, from basic operations like printing to the console and reading and writing files, to more advanced tasks like working with threads and networking.

Here is a list of some of the most commonly used built-in functions in Rust:

- **println!**: This function is used to print a message to the console, followed by a newline character.

- **print!**: This function is similar to println!, but it does not print a newline character at the end of the message.

- **format!**: This function is used to format a string using a special syntax called a "format string".

- **file::read_to_string**: This function is used to read the contents of a file into a string.

- **file::write_all**: This function is used to write a string to a file.

- **thread::spawn**: This function is used to create a new thread.

- **thread::sleep**: This function is used to sleep the current thread for a given amount of time.

- **net::TcpStream::connect**: This function is used to create a new TCP connection.

- **vec!**: This macro is used to create a new vector with a given set of elements.

- **String::new**: This function is used to create a new empty string.

- **String::push_str**: This function is used to append a string to the end of an existing string.

- **str::split**: This function is used to split a string into a vector of substrings based on a delimiter.

- **slice::join**: This function is used to join a slice of strings into a single string, using a delimiter.

- **hashmap::new**: This function is used to create a new empty hash map.

- **hashmap::insert**: This function is used to insert a key-value pair into a hash map.

- **hashmap::get**: This function is used to retrieve the value associated with a key in a hash map.

- **result::unwrap**: This function is used to unwrap the value of a Result type, returning the value if the Result is Ok or panicking if the Result is Err.

Control Flow

Control flow refers to the way that a program executes a sequence of statements based on certain conditions. Rust provides several control flow constructs that allow you to control the flow of execution in your program. Control flow constructs are an essential part of any programming language, as they allow you to create programs that can make decisions and execute different actions based on certain conditions.

In Rust, control flow constructs provide several benefits:

- Readability: Control flow constructs allow you to organize your code in a logical and easy-to-read way, which can make your programs easier to understand and maintain.

- Flexibility: Control flow constructs allow you to write programs that can adapt to different inputs and conditions, making them more flexible and adaptable.

- Performance: Rust's control flow constructs are optimized for performance, allowing you to write efficient programs that can make the most of the available resources.

Overall, control flow constructs are an important part of Rust that allow you to write powerful and flexible programs.

If Statements

The if keyword is used to create simple conditional tests. It can be used in conjuction with the else if and else keyword.

```rust
use rand::Rng;

fn main() {

    let mut rng = rand::thread_rng();

    let n = rng.gen_range(-5..5);

    if n < 0 {
        println!("negative value");
    } else if n == 0 {
        println!("zero");
    } else {
        println!("positive value");
    }
}
```

We randomly select a value from a range -5..5. Based on the resulting value, we print a message. There are three possible branches that can be executed.

```rust
if n < 0 {
    println!("negative value");
...
```

If the expression following the if keyword is true, the next statement is executed. Other branches are not executed.

```rust
} else if n == 0 {
    println!("zero");
...
```

If the previous branch was not true, we try the next branch; the else if. If it is true, it's block is executed and the testing is finished. If not, we continue to the next branch.

```rust
} else {
    println!("positive value");
```

```
}
```

The else branch is always executed when the previous ones fail.

Loop Statements

An infinite loop is created with the loop keyword. The loop is terminated with the break
keyword.

```
fn main() {
    let mut i = 0;

    loop {
        println!("falcon");

        i += 1;
        if i == 5 {
            break;
        }
    }
}
```

In the example, we print a word five times.

```
let mut i = 0;
```

We define a counter; the i is often used as a variable for a counter.

```
loop {
    println!("falcon");

    i += 1;
    if i == 5 {
        break;
    }
```

```
}
```

With loop, we start executing the given code block until we break the loop.

```
if i == 5 {
    break;
}
```

If the condition is met, the loop is terminated with break.

While Statements

The while keyword is used to create a loop. It runs until the given condition is met.

```
fn main() {
    let mut x = 1;

    while x <= 10 {
        println!("{}", x);
        x += 1;
    }

    println!("x: {}", x);
}
```

In the program, we print numbers 1 through 10. In the end, we print the x, which is used as a counter.

```
while x <= 10 {
    println!("{}", x);
    x += 1;
}
```

The while loop is executed while the condition is true; that is, x is less than 10.

Let's take another example wherein we use a while loop to calculate a sum of integers.

```rust
use std::vec;

fn main() {
    let vals = vec![1, 2, 3, 4, 5, 6, 7, 8, 9, 10];

    let mut i = 0;
    let mut sum = 0;
    let n = vals.len();

    while i < n {
        sum += vals[i];
        i += 1;
    }

    println!("The sum is: {}", sum);
}
```

We have a vector of integers. Using while loop, we calculate the sum of the elements.

```rust
let mut i = 0;
let mut sum = 0;
let n = vals.len();
```

In order to calculate the sum, we need an index variable, the sum variable, and the length of the vector.

```rust
while i < n {
    sum += vals[i];
    i += 1;
}
```

In the while loop, we add the elements to the sum variable.

For Statements

With the for keyword, we iterate over a range or collection of values.

```
fn main() {
    for i in 1..=10 {
        print!("{} ", i);
    }

    println!();

    let vals = [1, 2, 3, 4, 5, 6, 7, 8, 9, 10];

    for e in vals {
        print!("{} ", e);
    }

    println!();
}
```

In the program, we iterate over a range of integers and an array of integers.

```
for i in 1..=10 {
    print!("{} ", i);
}
```

We go through the integers of a range; in each cycle, the i variable holds the current value. We print the value in the block.

```
let vals = [1, 2, 3, 4, 5, 6, 7, 8, 9, 10];

for e in vals {
    print!("{} ", e);
}
```

We have an array of integers; we go through the array element by element and print the values to the terminal.

Match Expression

Pattern matching is a powerful control flow construct that allows us to compare a value against a series of patterns and then execute code based on which pattern matches.

In match expressions, each option that is executed is called an arm.

```rust
fn main() {
    let grades = ["A", "B", "C", "D", "E", "F", "FX"];

    for grade in grades {
        match grade {
            "A" | "B" | "C" | "D" | "E" | "F" =>
println!("passed"),
            "FX" => println!("failed"),
            _ => println!("unknown")
        }
    }
}
```

We have an array of grades. We go through the array and print "passed" or "failed" for each value. This example uses a multiple option arm, which saves a lot of space. It is much shorter than using several if/else keywords.

Understanding Traits

A trait is a way to define a set of behaviors that a type can have. a trait is similar to an interface in other programming languages, but it is more powerful because it allows you to define both the behavior and the types of the arguments and return values.

Following is an example of a trait in Rust that defines a behavior for a type that can be compared for equality:

```rust
trait Eq {
    fn eq(&self, other: &Self) -> bool;
}
```

This trait, called Eq, defines a single method called eq that takes a reference to self and another reference to an instance of the same type, and returns a boolean value indicating whether the two instances are equal.

To implement this trait for a type, you would use the impl keyword and define the behavior of the eq method for that type. Let's take a look at the following example:

```rust
impl Eq for i32 {
    fn eq(&self, other: &i32) -> bool {
        *self == *other
    }
}
```

This implementation of the Eq trait for the i32 type defines the behavior of the eq method as a simple equality comparison.

You can then use the eq method on instances of the i32 type just like any other method:

```rust
let x = 5;
let y = 10;
assert!(x.eq(&y) == false);
```

Traits are an important feature of Rust that provide several benefits:

- Code reuse: Traits allow you to define common behaviors that can be implemented by multiple types, allowing you to reuse code and avoid duplication.

- Abstraction: Traits allow you to abstract over the behavior of a type, allowing you to write code that works with any type that implements the trait, without needing to know the specific details of the type.

- Type safety: Traits allow you to specify the types of the arguments and return values for a behavior, ensuring that your code is type safe and that you can't pass the wrong types of arguments to a function.

- Dynamic dispatch: Traits can be used to implement dynamic dispatch, which allows you to write code that works with multiple types at runtime, rather than at compile-time.

Overall, traits are a powerful and flexible feature of Rust that allow you to write reusable, abstract, and type-safe code.

Types of Traits

There are several types of traits in Rust, each with its own specific purpose and behavior. Here are some of the most common types of traits:

- Behavioral traits: These traits define a set of behaviors that a type can have. For example, the Eq trait defined in the previous example is a behavioral trait, as it defines the behavior of comparing two values for equality.

- Inheritance traits: These traits allow you to define a type as a subtype of another type, allowing you to use the parent type's methods and behavior. For example, the std::error::Error trait allows a type to be treated as an error, and the std::fmt::Debug trait allows a type to be printed using the {:?} format string.

- Associated types: These traits define a placeholder type that is associated with the trait and can be used as a type parameter in the trait's methods. For example, the Iterator trait defines an associated type called Item, which represents the type of the elements that the iterator returns.

- Type bounds: These traits allow you to specify a requirement that a type must implement a certain trait in order to be used in a particular context. For example, the std::cmp::PartialEq trait allows you to specify that a type must implement the Eq trait in order to be compared for equality.

Implement Traits

To implement a trait for a type in Rust, you use the impl keyword and specify the trait name and the type that you are implementing it for. You can then define the behavior of the trait's methods for that type.

Following is an example of how to implement a trait for a simple Point struct:

```rust
struct Point {
    x: i32,
    y: i32,
}

trait Distance {
    fn distance(&self, other: &Self) -> f64;
}

impl Distance for Point {
    fn distance(&self, other: &Point) -> f64 {
        let dx = (other.x - self.x) as f64;
        let dy = (other.y - self.y) as f64;
        (dx * dx + dy * dy).sqrt()
    }
}
```

This code defines a Point struct with x and y fields, and a Distance trait with a single method called distance that calculates the distance between two Point instances.

The impl block then implements the Distance trait for the Point type, defining the behavior of the distance method as the Euclidean distance between the two points.

You can then use the distance method on instances of the Point type just like any other method:

```rust
let p1 = Point { x: 0, y: 0 };
let p2 = Point { x: 3, y: 4 };
```

```rust
let d = p1.distance(&p2);
println!("The distance between p1 and p2 is {}", d);
```

This code will print "The distance between p1 and p2 is 5.0" to the console.

Consider putting this additional example of how to build a trait in Rust to the test:

```rust
struct Rectangle {
    width: u32,
    height: u32,
}

trait HasArea {
    fn area(&self) -> u32;
}

impl HasArea for Rectangle {
    fn area(&self) -> u32 {
        self.width * self.height
    }
}

fn print_area<T: HasArea>(shape: T) {
    println!("The area is {}", shape.area());
}

fn main() {
    let rect = Rectangle { width: 10, height: 20 };
    print_area(rect);
}
```

This code defines a Rectangle struct with width and height fields, and a HasArea trait with a single method called area that calculates the area of the rectangle.

The impl block then implements the HasArea trait for the Rectangle type, defining the behavior of the area method as the product of the width and height fields.

The print_area function is a generic function that takes a type T that implements the HasArea trait as its argument and prints the area of the shape to the console.

In the main function, the program creates an instance of the Rectangle struct and calls the print_area function with it as the argument. The output of the program is:

```
The area is 200
```

Do's and Don'ts of Using Trait

Following are some tips for using traits in Rust:

Do:
- Use traits to define common behaviors that can be implemented by multiple types.
- Use associated types to define placeholder types that are associated with the trait and can be used as type parameters in the trait's methods.
- Use type bounds to specify requirements that a type must implement a certain trait in order to be used in a particular context.
- Use the impl keyword to implement a trait for a type.

Don't:
- Don't define a trait with only one method, as this is equivalent to a type alias. Instead, use a type alias or an associated type.
- Don't use a trait as a type. Instead, use a type that implements the trait.
- Don't use a trait as a function argument or return type. Instead, use a type that implements the trait.
- Don't define a trait with a method that takes self as a mutable reference, as this can lead to confusing and error-prone code.

Unions

A union is a type that represents a value that can take on multiple forms, but only one form at a time. Unions are similar to structs, but they take up less space in memory because they only store the largest field of the union, rather than all fields.

Following is an example of how to define a union in Rust:

```rust
union MyUnion {
    i: i32,
    f: f32,
}
```

This code defines a union called MyUnion with two fields, i and f, which are an i32 and an f32 respectively.

You can then create an instance of the union and access its fields using unsafe code:

```rust
let mut u = MyUnion { i: 10 };
unsafe {
    println!("u.i = {}", u.i);
    u.f = 3.14;
    println!("u.f = {}", u.f);
}
```

This code will print "u.i = 10" and "u.f = 3.14" to the console.

Note that accessing the fields of a union is unsafe because it can lead to data races and undefined behavior if the union is being accessed concurrently from multiple threads.

Types of Unions

There are several types of unions that you can define in Rust, depending on the types of the fields that you want to include in the union.

Here are some examples of different types of unions:

- Primitive types: You can define a union with fields of primitive types, such as integers, floating-point numbers, and boolean values. Let's take a look at the following example:

```rust
union MyUnion {
    i: i32,
```

```
    f: f32,
    b: bool,
}
```

- Enumerations: You can define a union with fields that are variants of an enumeration. Let's take a look at the following example:

```
enum Color {
    Red,
    Green,
    Blue,
}

union MyUnion {
    c: Color,
    i: i32,
}
```

- Structs: You can define a union with fields that are structs. Let's take a look at the following example:

```
struct Point {
    x: i32,
    y: i32,
}

union MyUnion {
    p: Point,
    i: i32,
}
```

- Arrays: You can define a union with fields that are arrays. Let's take a look at the following example:

```
union MyUnion {
    a: [i32; 4],
```

```
    i: i32,
}
```

Implementing Unions

To implement a union in Rust, you can follow these steps:

Define the union using the union keyword and the name of the union, followed by a block of curly braces containing the fields of the union. The fields can be any valid Rust types, such as primitive types, enumerations, structs, or arrays.

The following is an illustration of how to define a union using only primitive types:

```
union MyUnion {
    i: i32,
    f: f32,
}
```

Create an instance of the union using the fields of the union as arguments to the union's constructor. Let's take a look at the following example:

```
let u = MyUnion { i: 10 };
```

Access the fields of the union using unsafe code. Let's take a look at the following example:

```
unsafe {
    println!("u.i = {}", u.i);
}
```

Note that accessing the fields of a union is unsafe because it can lead to data races and undefined behavior if the union is being accessed concurrently from multiple threads.

Modify the fields of the union using unsafe code. Let's take a look at the following example:

```
unsafe {
```

```rust
    u.f = 3.14;
}
```

Finding it difficult to understand? Here is a more complete example of how to implement a union in Rust:

```rust
union MyUnion {
    i: i32,
    f: f32,
}

fn main() {
    // Create an instance of the union with the `i`
field set to 10
    let mut u = MyUnion { i: 10 };

    // Access and print the value of the `i` field
    unsafe {
        println!("u.i = {}", u.i);
    }

    // Modify the value of the `f` field
    unsafe {
        u.f = 3.14;
    }

    // Access and print the value of the `f` field
    unsafe {
        println!("u.f = {}", u.f);
    }
}
```

This code defines a union called MyUnion with two fields, i and f, which are an i32 and an f32 respectively.

The program then creates an instance of the union with the i field set to 10, and uses unsafe code to access and print the value of the i field. The output is:

```
u.i = 10
```

The program then uses unsafe code to modify the value of the f field to 3.14, and uses unsafe code to access and print the value of the f field. The output is:

```
u.f = 3.14
```

CHAPTER 4: STRUCTS

Understanding Structs

A struct is a composite data type that lets you store several values of different types as a single entity. Structs are useful when you need to define a custom data type to represent a specific concept in your program. to define a struct in Rust, you use the struct keyword followed by the name of the struct and a set of fields enclosed in curly braces.

Following is an example of a struct definition in Rust:

```rust
struct Point {
    x: i32,
    y: i32,
}
```

This defines a struct called Point that has two fields: x and y, both of which are i32 (32-bit signed integer) values.

To create a new instance of a struct, you can use the new function, like this:

```rust
let p = Point { x: 10, y: 20 };
```

You can also define methods on structs, which are functions that are associated with the struct and can be called on its instances. Following is an example of a method defined on the Point struct:

```rust
struct Point {
    x: i32,
    y: i32,
}

impl Point {
    fn distance_from_origin(&self) -> f64 {
        let x = self.x as f64;
        let y = self.y as f64;
        (x*x + y*y).sqrt()
    }
```

```
}
```

This method calculates the distance of the point from the origin (0, 0) and returns it as a f64 value. The &self parameter is a reference to the struct instance on which the method is being called, and it's a convention in Rust to use it as the first parameter in methods defined on structs.

You can call this method on a Point instance like this:

```
let p = Point { x: 10, y: 20 };
let distance = p.distance_from_origin();
```

Structs are a useful feature in Rust programming that allow you to define custom data types with a set of named fields. Structs can be used to represent complex data structures, such as a point in 3D space or a player in a video game.

Following are the benefits of using structs in Rust include:

- Encapsulation: Structs allow you to group related data together and hide implementation details from other parts of the code, making it easier to reason about and manage the data.

- Code reuse: You can reuse structs by creating multiple instances of them, which can be particularly useful when working with large data sets or when defining common data structures that will be used in multiple places in your code.

- Type safety: Rust's type system helps ensure that you are using structs correctly and helps prevent common programming errors.

- Performance: Structs can be more efficient than alternatives such as hash maps or arrays, especially when the data being stored is small and simple.

Overall, structs are a powerful and flexible tool for organizing and manipulating data in Rust, and they can help you write more readable and maintainable code.

Types of Structs

There are several different types of structs in Rust:

1. Tuple structs: These are structs that consist of a fixed number of fields, each with a different type. Tuple structs are often used when you want to give a group of values a name, but don't need to store any additional data or behavior.

2. Unit structs: These are structs that do not have any fields. Unit structs are often used as a placeholder or as a type in generic code.

3. Structs with named fields: These are structs that have a fixed number of fields, each with a name and a type. Structs with named fields are the most common type of struct in Rust and are often used to represent more complex data structures.

4. Dynamically sized structs: These are structs that can have an arbitrary number of fields, such as a linked list or a tree. Dynamically sized structs are implemented using a feature called "Dynamically Sized Types" (DSTs), which allows the size of the struct to be determined at runtime.

In addition to these types of structs, Rust also supports a variety of other advanced features for working with structs, such as inheritance, polymorphism, and trait implementations.

Writing Program Using Struct

Following is an example of a struct in Rust that could be used to represent a student in a school database:

```
struct Student {
    id: i32,
    name: String,
    major: String,
    year: i32,
}
```

we define a struct called Student that represents a student in a school database. The Student struct has four fields:

1. id: This field is an integer that represents the student's unique identifier. It could be used to look up the student's record in the database or to distinguish one student from another.

2. name: This field is a string that contains the student's name. It could be used to display the student's name on a report or to personalize communication with the student.

3. major: This field is a string that contains the student's major field of study. It could be used to group students by major or to determine which classes a student should take.

4. year: This field is an integer that represents the student's current year in school. It could be used to track a student's progress through the program or to determine their eligibility for certain opportunities or privileges.

You could then use this struct to create instances representing individual students, like this:

```
let s1 = Student { id: 1, name: "Alice".to_string(),
major: "Computer Science".to_string(), year: 3 };
let s2 = Student { id: 2, name: "Bob".to_string(),
major: "Physics".to_string(), year: 4 };
let s3 = Student { id: 3, name: "Charlie".to_string(),
major: "Chemistry".to_string(), year: 2 };
```

To create instances of the Student struct, we use the Student syntax followed by a set of curly braces containing field names and values. This creates a new Student instance with an id of 1, a name of "Alice", a major of "Computer Science", and a year of 3.

You could then use these struct instances to store and manipulate data about the students in your program. For example, you could define a method on the Student struct to calculate the GPA of a student based on their grades, or you could create a function to search for students with a particular major.

```
impl Student {
    fn calculate_gpa(&self, grades: &[i32]) -> f64 {
        let sum: i32 = grades.iter().sum();
        let num_grades = grades.len() as f64;
        sum as f64 / num_grades
    }
```

}

Then type,

```
let s1_gpa = s1.calculate_gpa(&[90, 95, 80]);
```

This would calculate the GPA of the s1 student based on their grades and return the result.

Custom Structs

Custom structs are structs that you define yourself in your Rust code, rather than using one of the built-in structs provided by the standard library. They are useful when you need to represent a data structure that does not fit one of the built-in structs, or when you want to define a struct with specific behavior or functionality.

To define a custom struct in Rust, you use the struct keyword followed by the name of the struct and a set of fields enclosed in curly braces. Let's take a look at the following example:

```
struct Person {
    name: String,
    age: u8,
}
```

This defines a struct called Person with two fields: name, which is a string containing the person's name, and age, which is an unsigned 8-bit integer representing the person's age.

You can then create instances of the Person struct using the new function or the shorthand syntax:

```
let p1 = Person { name: "Alice".to_string(), age: 30 };
let p2 = Person { name: "Bob".to_string(), age: 40 };
```

You can also define methods on a struct by using the impl keyword, like this:

```
impl Person {
```

```rust
    fn say_hello(&self) {
        println!("Hello, my name is {} and I am {}
years old", self.name, self.age);
    }
}
```

You can then call this method on an instance of the Person struct like this:

```rust
p1.say_hello();
```

It's also possible to define methods that take other parameters in addition to self, as well as associated functions that do not take a self parameter.

Custom structs are an important tool for organizing and manipulating data in Rust and can help you write more readable and maintainable code. I hope this helps to clarify how to program custom structs in Rust!

Writing Custom Struct Program

Following is an example of a custom struct in Rust that represents a rectangle:

```rust
struct Rectangle {
    width: u32,
    height: u32,
}
```

This struct has two fields: width, which is an unsigned 32-bit integer representing the width of the rectangle, and height, which is an unsigned 32-bit integer representing the height of the rectangle.

You can create instances of the Rectangle struct using the new function or the shorthand syntax:

```rust
let r1 = Rectangle { width: 10, height: 20 };
let r2 = Rectangle { width: 5, height: 15 };
```

You can then access the fields of a Rectangle instance using the dot notation, like this:

```rust
println!("The width of r1 is {}", r1.width);
println!("The height of r1 is {}", r1.height);
```

You can also define methods on the Rectangle struct to add behavior or functionality to the struct. For example, you could define a method to calculate the area of a rectangle like this:

```rust
impl Rectangle {
    fn area(&self) -> u32 {
        self.width * self.height
    }
}
```

You can then call this method on a Rectangle instance like this:

```rust
let r1_area = r1.area();
```

It's also possible to define associated functions, which are functions that are associated with a struct but do not take a self parameter. For example, you could define a function to create a new Rectangle with a given width and height like this:

```rust
impl Rectangle {
    fn new(width: u32, height: u32) -> Rectangle {
        Rectangle { width, height }
    }
}
```

You can then call this function to create a new Rectangle instance like this:

```rust
let r3 = Rectangle::new(30, 40);
```

Overall, custom structs are a powerful tool for organizing and manipulating data in Rust and can help you write more readable and maintainable code.

Writing a Nested Structs

A nested struct is a struct that is defined inside another struct. Nested structs are often used when a data structure is closely related to the struct it is nested within, or when the nested struct is only used in the context of the outer struct.

To define a nested struct in Rust, you can use the struct keyword followed by the name of the nested struct and a set of fields enclosed in curly braces, like this:

```rust
struct OuterStruct {
    field1: i32,
    field2: i32,
    nested: InnerStruct,
}

struct InnerStruct {
    field3: i32,
    field4: i32,
}
```

In the given example, the OuterStruct struct has two fields, field1 and field2, as well as a field called nested of type InnerStruct. The InnerStruct struct has two fields, field3 and field4.

You can create instances of the nested struct using the new function or the shorthand syntax:

```rust
let inner = InnerStruct { field3: 10, field4: 20 };
let outer = OuterStruct { field1: 1, field2: 2, nested: inner };
```

You can then access the fields of the nested struct using the dot notation, like this:

```rust
println!("The value of field3 is {}",
outer.nested.field3);
```

```rust
println!("The value of field4 is {}",
outer.nested.field4);
```

You can also define methods on the nested struct using the impl keyword, like this:

```rust
impl InnerStruct {
    fn sum(&self) -> i32 {
        self.field3 + self.field4
    }
}
```

You can then call this method on an instance of the nested struct like this:

```rust
let inner_sum = outer.nested.sum();
```

Nested structs are a useful tool for organizing data in Rust and can help you write more readable and maintainable code.

Struct Inheritance In Rust

Struct inheritance is a feature in some programming languages that allows one struct to inherit the fields and methods of another struct. In Rust, struct inheritance is not directly supported, but there are several ways to achieve similar functionality.

One way to achieve struct inheritance-like behavior in Rust is to use composition, which involves defining a struct that contains an instance of another struct as one of its fields. Let's take a look at the following example:

```rust
struct BaseStruct {
    field1: i32,
    field2: i32,
}

struct DerivedStruct {
    base: BaseStruct,
```

```
    field3: i32,
}
```

In the given example, the DerivedStruct struct has a field called base of type BaseStruct, which allows it to access the fields and methods of the BaseStruct.

You can then create instances of the DerivedStruct struct using the new function or the shorthand syntax:

```
let base = BaseStruct { field1: 1, field2: 2 };
let derived = DerivedStruct { base, field3: 3 };
```

You can access the fields of the BaseStruct within the DerivedStruct using the dot notation, like this:

```
println!("The value of field1 is {}",
derived.base.field1);
println!("The value of field2 is {}",
derived.base.field2);
```

You can also define methods on the BaseStruct and call them from the DerivedStruct, like this:

```
impl BaseStruct {
    fn sum(&self) -> i32 {
        self.field1 + self.field2
    }
}

let base_sum = derived.base.sum();
```

Another way to achieve struct inheritance-like behavior in Rust is to use trait objects, which allow you to define a type that can represent multiple types that implement a particular trait. You can then define a struct that contains a trait object field, which allows it to access the methods defined by the trait. Let's take a look at the following example:

```rust
trait BaseTrait {
    fn sum(&self) -> i32;
}

struct DerivedStruct<'a> {
    base: &'a BaseTrait,
    field3: i32,
}
```

In the given example, the DerivedStruct struct has a field called base of type &BaseTrait, which is a trait object that can represent any type that implements the BaseTrait trait. The DerivedStruct can then access the sum method defined by the trait.

You can then create instances of the DerivedStruct struct using the new function or the shorthand syntax:

```rust
struct BaseStruct {
    field1: i32,
    field2: i32,
}

impl BaseTrait for BaseStruct {
    fn sum(&self) -> i32 {
        self.field1
```

Do's and Don'ts of Struct

Here are some do's and don'ts to consider when using structs in Rust:

Do's:
- Do use structs to represent data structures that have a fixed set of fields with well-defined types.
- Do use named fields in your structs to make the purpose of each field clear.
- Do use methods to add behavior or functionality to your structs.
- Do use associated functions to define functions that are associated with your structs but do not take a self parameter.

- Do use impl blocks to define methods and associated functions for your structs.
- Do consider using nested structs or composition when you want to reuse fields or methods across multiple structs.
- Do consider using trait objects when you want to define a type that can represent multiple types that implement a particular trait.

Don'ts:

- Don't use structs to represent data structures that have a variable number of fields or fields with varying types. In these cases, consider using an enum with variant types instead.
- Don't use anonymous fields in your structs unless it is necessary for the purpose of the struct. Anonymous fields can make it harder to understand the purpose of each field.
- Don't define methods that mutate the fields of your structs unless it is necessary for the purpose of the struct. Consider using &self instead of &mut self to define methods that do not mutate the struct.
- Don't define methods or associated functions that have side effects unless it is necessary for the purpose of the struct.
- Don't define methods or associated functions that return references to fields of the struct unless you are sure that the returned reference will not outlive the lifetime of the struct.
- Don't define methods or associated functions that panic unless it is necessary for the purpose of the struct.

CHAPTER 5: ENUMS AND PATTERN MATCHING

Defining Enum

An enum, which is an abbreviation for "enumeration," is a type that can take on a predetermined list of values. These values are referred to as the type's "variants." Enumerations are frequently utilised to depict a limited number of available choices or states.

You could build an enum, for instance, to represent the four different suits that come with a deck of cards:

```
enum Suit {
    Spades,
    Hearts,
    Diamonds,
    Clubs,
}
```

Each variant of the Suit enum can be used as a value of the Suit type. You can create a value of the Suit type by specifying one of the variants, like this:

```
let my_suit = Suit::Spades;
```

You can also define enum variants that have associated data. For example, you might define an enum to represent the possible values of a playing card:

```
enum Card {
    Ace(Suit),
    Two(Suit),
    Three(Suit),
    // ...
}
```

Each variant of the Card enum has a single associated value of type Suit. You can create a value of the Card type by specifying the variant and the associated data, like this:

```rust
let my_card = Card::Ace(Suit::Spades);
```

Pattern Matching

Pattern matching is a feature in Rust that allows you to write code that can execute different branches depending on the variant of an enum value. You can use pattern matching to compare an enum value to a list of patterns, and execute different code for each pattern.

Following is an example of using pattern matching with an enum:

```rust
let my_suit = Suit::Spades;

match my_suit {
    Suit::Spades => println!("The suit is spades"),
    Suit::Hearts => println!("The suit is hearts"),
    Suit::Diamonds => println!("The suit is diamonds"),
    Suit::Clubs => println!("The suit is clubs"),
}
```

In the given example, the match expression compares the value of my_suit to each of the patterns in the match arms. If the value of my_suit matches a particular pattern, the code in the corresponding match arm will be executed. In this case, if my_suit is Suit::Spades, the code println!("The suit is spades") will be executed.

You can also use pattern matching to destructure enum values with associated data. Let's take a look at the following example:

```rust
let my_card = Card::Ace(Suit::Spades);

match my_card {
    Card::Ace(suit) => println!("The card is an ace of
{}", suit),
    Card::Two(suit) => println!("The card is a two of
{}", suit),
```

```
    Card::Three(suit) => println!("The card is a three
of {}", suit),
    // ...
}
```

In the given example, the match expression compares the value of my_card to each of the patterns in the match arms. If the value of my_card matches a particular pattern, the code in the corresponding match arm will be executed, and the associated data will be bound to the pattern variable suit.

Advantage of Enum and Pattern Matching

Enums and pattern matching provide several benefits in Rust:

- Type safety: Enums allow you to define a fixed set of values for a type, which can help prevent the kind of runtime errors that can occur when working with "magic numbers" or string constants.

- Readability: Enums can make your code more self-explanatory, especially when used in combination with pattern matching. For example, consider the following code:

```
enum HttpStatus {
    Ok,
    NotFound,
    InternalServerError,
}

fn handle_request(status: HttpStatus) {
    match status {
        HttpStatus::Ok => println!("Request
succeeded"),
        HttpStatus::NotFound => println!("Resource not
found"),
        HttpStatus::InternalServerError => println!("An
internal server error occurred"),
    }
```

```
}
```

In this code, the enum and pattern matching make it clear what each possible value of status represents, and what should happen in each case. This can make the code easier to understand, especially for someone who is not familiar with the codebase.

- Concise code: Enums and pattern matching can also help you write more concise code, especially when working with large data structures or multiple branches of conditional logic. For example, consider the following code:

```
struct Person {
    age: u8,
    job: Option<String>,
}

fn classify_person(person: Person) ->&'static str {
    if person.age < 18 {
        return "Minor";
    } else if person.age < 65 {
        return "Adult";
    } else {
        return "Senior";
    }
}
```

This code uses an if-else chain to classify a person based on their age. You could rewrite this code using an enum and pattern matching like this:

```
enum AgeCategory {
    Minor,
    Adult,
    Senior,
}

fn classify_person(person: Person) -> AgeCategory {
    match person.age {
        age if age < 18 => AgeCategory::Minor,
```

```
            age if age < 65 => AgeCategory::Adult,
            _ => AgeCategory::Senior,
        }
    }
}
```

This version of the code uses a match expression to classify the person, which can make the code more concise and easier to read.

- Efficiency: Enums and pattern matching can also be more efficient than using if-else chains, especially when working with large data structures or multiple branches of conditional logic. In Rust, the compiler is able to optimize enum values and pattern matching more effectively than it can optimize if-else chains, which can result in faster code.

Writing a Program For Enum From Scratch

The following piece of code classifies a person according to their age by making use of an enum and pattern matching:

```
enum AgeCategory {
    Minor,
    Adult,
    Senior,
}

struct Person {
    age: u8,
    job: Option<String>,
}

fn classify_person(person: Person) -> AgeCategory {
    match person.age {
        age if age < 18 => AgeCategory::Minor,
        age if age < 65 => AgeCategory::Adult,
        _ => AgeCategory::Senior,
    }
```

```rust
}

fn main() {
    let p1 = Person { age: 17, job: None };
    let p2 = Person { age: 35, job: Some("Software
engineer".to_string()) };
    let p3 = Person { age: 70, job:
Some("Retired".to_string()) };

    println!("{:?} is a {:?}", p1.job,
classify_person(p1));
    println!("{:?} is a {:?}", p2.job,
classify_person(p2));
    println!("{:?} is a {:?}", p3.job,
classify_person(p3));
}
```

In the given example, the AgeCategory enum has three variants: Minor, Adult, and Senior. The classify_person function takes a Person struct as input and returns an AgeCategory value using a match expression. The match expression compares the value of the age field of the Person struct to a list of patterns, and returns the corresponding AgeCategory variant for each pattern.

In the main function, we create three Person values with different ages and jobs, and pass each one to the classify_person function. The classify_person function returns an AgeCategory value for each person, which is then printed using the println! macro.

Running this program would output the following:

```
None is a Minor
Some("Software engineer") is a Adult
Some("Retired") is a Senior
```

Advanced Aspects of 'match' Expression

There are several advanced aspects of pattern matching in Rust that you might find useful:

- Matching on multiple patterns: You can use the | operator to match on multiple patterns at the same time. Let's take a look at the following example:

```
let x = 3;

match x {
    1 | 2 | 3 => println!("x is 1, 2, or 3"),
    _ => println!("x is something else"),
}
```

In the given example, the match expression will match on the patterns 1, 2, and 3, and will execute the code in the first match arm if x is any of those values.

- Matching on ranges: You can use the .. operator to match on a range of values. Let's take a look at the following example:

```
let x = 3;

match x {
    1..=5 => println!("x is between 1 and 5"),
    _ => println!("x is something else"),
}
```

In the given example, the match expression will match on the range 1..=5, and will execute the code in the first match arm if x is any value in that range.

- Matching on a reference: You can use the & operator to match on a reference to a value. Let's take a look at the following example:

```
let x = 3;

match &x {
    &y if y > 3 => println!("x is a reference to a
value greater than 3"),
```

```rust
        &y if y < 3 => println!("x is a reference to a
value less than 3"),
        _ => println!("x is a reference to a value equal to
3"),
}
```

In the given example, the match expression will match on the reference &x, and will execute the code in the first or second match arm depending on the value that the reference points to.

- Matching on a destructured value: You can use pattern matching to destructively assign the fields of a struct or the elements of a tuple to variables. Let's take a look at the following example:

```rust
struct Point {
    x: i32,
    y: i32,
}

let p = Point { x: 3, y: 4 };

match p {
    Point { x, y } => println!("x: {}, y: {}", x, y),
}
```

In the given example, the match expression destructures the Point value p into its x and y fields, and binds those fields to the variables x and y.

- Matching on a type: You can use the is operator to match on the type of a value. Let's take a look at the following example:

```rust
let x = 3;

match x {
    x if x is i32 => println!("x is an i32"),
    _ => println!("x is something else"),
}
```

In the given example, the match expression will match on the type of x, and will execute the code in the first match arm if x is an i32.

```
let x = 3;

match x {
    1..=5 => println!("x is between 1 and 5"),
    _ => println!("x is something else"),
}
```

Matching on a guard: You can use a guard clause to specify additional conditions that a pattern must meet in order to match. a guard clause is a boolean expression that is placed after the pattern, separated by a `

Following is an example of using a guard clause in a match expression:

```
let x = 3;

match x {
    y if y % 2 == 0 => println!("x is even"),
    y if y % 2 == 1 => println!("x is odd"),
    _ => println!("x is something else"),
}
```

In the given example, the match expression has two patterns, each with a guard clause that checks whether the value of y is even or odd. If the value of y meets the conditions specified in the guard clause, the corresponding match arm will be executed.

You can also use a guard clause with a destructured value, like this:

```
struct Point {
    x: i32,
    y: i32,
}

let p = Point { x: 3, y: 4 };
```

```rust
match p {
    Point { x, y } if x < y => println!("x is less than
y"),
    Point { x, y } if x > y => println!("x is greater
than y"),
    _ => println!("x is equal to y"),
}
```

In the given example, the match expression has two patterns, each with a guard clause that
checks whether the value of x is less than or greater than the value of y. If the value of x
meets the conditions specified in the guard clause, the corresponding match arm will be
executed.

Using Control Flow

You can use if and else statements to control the flow of execution in your program when
working with enums and pattern matching. Following is an example of using if and else with
an enum:

```rust
enum HttpStatus {
    Ok,
    NotFound,
    InternalServerError,
}

fn handle_request(status: HttpStatus) {
    if let HttpStatus::Ok = status {
        println!("Request succeeded");
    } else if let HttpStatus::NotFound = status {
        println!("Resource not found");
    } else if let HttpStatus::InternalServerError =
status {
        println!("An internal server error occurred");
    } else {
        println!("Unknown status code");
    }
```

}

In the given example, the if let statement is used to check the value of the status variable against the HttpStatus::Ok variant. If the value of status is HttpStatus::Ok, the code in the first if block will be executed. If the value of status is not HttpStatus::Ok, the code in the second if let statement will be executed, and so on.

You can also use if and else statements with pattern matching to control the flow of execution based on the value of an enum with associated data:

```
enum Card {
    Ace(Suit),
    Two(Suit),
    Three(Suit),
    // ...
}

fn handle_card(card: Card) {
    if let Card::Ace(suit) = card {
        println!("The card is an ace of {}", suit);
    } else if let Card::Two(suit) = card {
        println!("The card is a two of {}", suit);
    } else if let Card::Three(suit) = card {
        println!("The card is a three of {}", suit);
    } else {
        println!("The card is something else");
    }
}
```

In the given example, the if let statements are used to check the value of the card variable against the different variants of the Card enum. If the value of card matches a particular variant, the code in the corresponding if block will be executed, and the associated data will be bound to the pattern variable suit.

Do's and Don'ts of Enum & Pattern Matching

Here are some do's and don'ts to keep in mind when working with enums and pattern matching in Rust:

Do:

- Use enums to represent a finite set of options or states.
- Use pattern matching to compare an enum value to a list of patterns and execute different code for each pattern.
- Use an _ catch-all pattern to handle cases that are not explicitly covered by other patterns.
- Use if let statements to match on a single pattern and execute code if the pattern matches.

Don't:

- Don't forget to include a catch-all pattern in your match expressions to handle cases that are not explicitly covered by other patterns. If you don't include a catch-all pattern, your code will panic at runtime if the value being matched does not match any of the other patterns.
- Don't use match expressions in performance-critical code without considering the performance implications. In some cases, using if-else chains or other control flow constructs may be more efficient.
- Don't use match expressions to perform side effects without returning a value. Instead, consider using a loop or while statement to perform the side effect repeatedly.

Chapter 6: Exploring Ownership and Borrowing

Concept of Ownership

In Rust, ownership is a system that the Rust compiler uses to ensure memory safety. The basic idea behind ownership is that every value in Rust has a variable that's called its owner, and that value is only valid as long as that owner is valid.

There are a few rules that govern ownership in Rust. These rules help ensure that values are always used in a valid and safe way, and they allow Rust to automatically manage the memory for you so you don't have to worry about things like dangling pointers or memory leaks.

One key concept related to ownership in Rust is that of borrowing. When you borrow a value, you are given a reference to that value, which allows you to read or modify the value without taking ownership of it. This is useful when you want to pass a value to a function or method without transferring ownership.

Characteristics of Ownership

- Ownership is a central feature of Rust's design.
- Every value in Rust has a single owner.
- When the owner goes out of scope, the value is dropped.
- Ownership is implemented using a system of stack-allocated variables and references.

Characteristics of Borrowing

- Borrowing allows you to use a value without taking ownership of it.
- You can have multiple borrows of a value at the same time, but you can only have one mutable borrow at a time.
- Borrows are implemented using references.
- Borrowing follows the same scoping rules as ownership.

Stack-allocated Variables and References

In Rust, stack-allocated variables are variables that are stored on the stack, which is a region of memory managed by the operating system. When you create a stack-allocated variable, the memory for that variable is automatically allocated and deallocated when the variable goes out of scope.

References, on the other hand, are values that refer to some other data. In Rust, references are used to refer to values that are stored on the stack or in the heap (which is a region of memory managed by the Rust runtime).

In the context of ownership, stack-allocated variables are used to hold the ownership of values, while references are used to borrow those values. For example, consider the following Rust code:

```rust
fn main() {
    let x = 5; // x is a stack-allocated variable with the value 5
    let y = &x; // y is a reference to x
}
```

In the given example, x is a stack-allocated variable with the value 5, and y is a reference to x. The & operator is used to create a reference to a value.

References are a key part of Rust's ownership system because they allow you to use a value without taking ownership of it. This is useful when you want to pass a value to a function or method without transferring ownership. Let's take a look at the following example:

```rust
fn add_one(x: &mut i32) {
    *x += 1;
}

fn main() {
    let mut x = 5;
    add_one(&mut x);
    println!("{}", x); // prints 6
}
```

In the given example, add_one is a function that takes a mutable reference to an i32 as an argument. The * operator is used to dereference the reference and access the underlying value. Since add_one takes a reference to x rather than ownership of x, x remains valid after the call to add_one, and the value is correctly printed as 6.

Applications of Ownership and Borrowing

Ownership and borrowing are important concepts for Rust developers because they help ensure memory safety and prevent common programming errors such as null or dangling pointer references.

Here are some examples of how ownership and borrowing can be useful for developers:

- Preventing null or dangling pointer references: By ensuring that every value has a single owner and that values are dropped when their owners go out of scope, Rust can prevent null or dangling pointer references, which can cause segmentation faults and other problems.

- Managing memory automatically: The Rust compiler can automatically manage the memory for you, so you don't have to worry about manually allocating and deallocating memory or worrying about memory leaks.

- Enabling safe concurrent programming: By allowing multiple borrows of a value at the same time, but only allowing one mutable borrow at a time, Rust's borrowing system enables safe concurrent programming. This can be useful for building high-performance, concurrent applications.

- Improving performance: Because Rust's ownership and borrowing system allows the compiler to make more optimization decisions, Rust programs can often run faster than programs written in other languages.

Overall, the ownership and borrowing system in Rust helps developers write safe, efficient, and concurrent code.

Libraries adopting Ownership and Borrowing

There are no libraries specifically related to ownership and borrowing in Rust, as these are fundamental concepts built into the language itself. However, there are a number of libraries that make use of Rust's ownership and borrowing system to provide various types of functionality.

Following are a few examples of libraries that make use of Rust's ownership and borrowing system:

- Smart pointers: Smart pointers are types that behave like regular pointers, but they have additional functionality such as automatic memory management and thread-safety. Examples of smart pointers in Rust include Box<T>, Rc<T>, and Arc<T>.

- Collections: Rust's standard library provides a number of collection types, such as vectors, linked lists, and hash maps, that make use of Rust's ownership and borrowing system to store and manage data.

- Concurrency libraries: Libraries such as std::sync::Mutex and std::sync::RwLock use Rust's borrowing system to provide thread-safe access to shared data.

Overall, Rust's ownership and borrowing system is a key part of the language, and it is used by many libraries to provide various types of functionality.

CHAPTER 7: CARGO, CRATES AND PACKAGES

Understanding Cargo

Cargo is the official package manager for the Rust programming language. It is used to manage Rust projects, including building, testing, and releasing Rust code.

Cargo has several features that make it easy to work with Rust projects:

- Crate dependencies: Cargo makes it easy to manage the dependencies of a Rust project. You can specify the dependencies of your project in a Cargo.toml file, and Cargo will automatically download and build the required crates (the Rust equivalent of libraries).

- Build automation: Cargo can build your Rust project and all of its dependencies with a single command. It will also automatically re-build your project and its dependencies if you make any changes to the code.

- Testing: Cargo makes it easy to run tests for your Rust project. You can use the cargo test command to run all of the tests in your project, or you can use the --test flag to run specific tests.

- Documentation generation: Cargo can generate documentation for your Rust project and its dependencies. You can use the cargo doc command to generate the documentation, and then view it in a web browser.

- Publishing: Cargo makes it easy to publish your Rust crates (libraries) to the official Rust package registry, crates.io. You can use the cargo publish command to publish your crate to crates.io, and then other users can use Cargo to include your crate as a dependency in their own projects.

Cargo is an essential tool for working with Rust projects, and it is included with the Rust installation by default.

Understanding Crates

In Rust, a crate is a unit of code that is compiled and packaged together. Crates can be libraries or executables, and they can be used to organize code and share it with other Rust projects.

There are two types of crates in Rust:

- Binary crates: Binary crates are crates that produce an executable when they are compiled. Binary crates have a main function, which is the entry point of the executable.

- Library crates: Library crates are crates that do not produce an executable when they are compiled. Instead, they contain functions, types, and other code that can be used by other crates. Library crates do not have a main function, and they are intended to be used as dependencies in other projects.

Crates are organized into a tree-like structure, with each crate depending on other crates that it uses. This allows you to modularize your code and reuse it across different projects.

Crates are managed with the Cargo package manager, which is the official package manager for Rust. You can use Cargo to build and test crates, generate documentation, and publish crates to the official Rust package registry, crates.io.

Understanding Packages

In Rust, a package is a collection of crates that are bundled together and managed as a single unit. a package typically contains one or more library crates and possibly one or more binary crates, as well as metadata such as the package name, version, and dependencies.

To create a package in Rust, you need to create a Cargo.toml file in the root directory of your project. This file contains metadata about your package, including the package name, version, and dependencies. You can also specify the crates that are included in your package in the Cargo.toml file.

Following is an example of a simple Cargo.toml file for a Rust package:

```
[package]
name = "my-package"
version = "0.1.0"
authors = ["Alice <alice@example.com>"]

[dependencies]
my-crate = "0.2.0"
```

In the given example, the package is called "my-package" and has a version of "0.1.0". It has one dependency, a crate called "my-crate" with a version of "0.2.0".

Creating My First Crate

To create a new crate in Rust with the name "helpcode", you can use the cargo new command. This command creates a new Rust project and generates the necessary files and directories for you.

To create a new crate called "helpcode", you can use the following command:

```
cargo new helpcode --lib
```

This command will create a new Rust project in a directory called "helpcode", and it will generate a library crate. The --lib flag specifies that the crate should be a library crate, rather than a binary crate.

The cargo new command will generate the following files and directories:

```
helpcode/
├── Cargo.toml
└── src/
    └── lib.rs
```

The Cargo.toml file is the manifest file for the crate, and it contains metadata about the crate, such as the crate name, version, and dependencies. The src/lib.rs file is the source code file for the crate.

Once the crate is created, you can add code to the src/lib.rs file and use Cargo to build and test the crate. You can also use Cargo to generate documentation for the crate and publish it to the official Rust package registry, crates.io.

After creating a new crate with cargo new, there are several steps you can take to continue developing and working with your crate:

- Add code to the crate: You can add code to the src/lib.rs file to define functions, types, and other code that will be part of your crate. You can also add additional source code files to the src directory if you want to organize your code into multiple files.

- Build the crate: You can use the cargo build command to build the crate. This will compile the crate and its dependencies, and produce a compiled version of the crate.

- Run tests: If you have added test functions to your crate, you can use the cargo test command to run the tests. This will compile and run the tests, and print the test results to the console.

- Generate documentation: You can use the cargo doc command to generate documentation for your crate. This will generate documentation for the crate and its dependencies, and create an HTML version of the documentation that you can view in a web browser.

- Publish the crate: If you want to share your crate with other users, you can use the cargo publish command to publish the crate to the official Rust package registry, crates.io. This will make the crate available for other users to include as a dependency in their own projects.

Build My First Package

To build a package in Rust after creating the crates, you can use the cargo build command. This command will build the package and all of its dependencies, and create a compiled version of the package.

Following is an example of how to use the cargo build command:

```
cargo build
```

This command will build the package and produce a compiled version of the package in the target directory. The compiled version of the package will be a binary file, which can be run as an executable.

If you want to build the package in release mode, which optimizes the code for performance, you can use the --release flag:

```
cargo build --release
```

This command will build the package in release mode, and produce a compiled version of the package in the target/release directory.

You can also use the cargo check command to perform a quick check of the package without building the entire package. This can be useful if you want to verify that the package builds without actually building it.

Publish the Package

To turn a crate into a package and publish it to the official Rust package registry, crates.io, you can use the cargo publish command. This command will package the crate and its dependencies, and publish it to crates.io, making it available for other users to include as a dependency in their own projects.

Following is an example of how to use the cargo publish command:

```
cargo publish
```

This command will package the crate and its dependencies, and publish the package to crates.io.

Before you can use the cargo publish command, you will need to create an account on crates.io and authenticate with the cargo login command. You will also need to specify the package name and version in the Cargo.toml file for the crate.

Following is an example of a Cargo.toml file for a Rust package:

```
[package]
name = "helpcode"
version = "0.1.0"
authors = ["Alice <alice@example.com>"]

[dependencies]
my-crate = "0.2.0"
```

In the given example, the package is called "helpcode" and has a version of "0.1.0". It has one dependency, a crate called "my-crate" with a version of "0.2.0".

Role of Modules and Paths In Rust

In Rust, modules are used to organize code and control visibility. Modules allow you to divide your code into smaller, more manageable pieces, and you can use them to control which parts of your code are visible to other parts of your code.

Modules in Rust are defined using the mod keyword, and they are typically stored in their own source code files. For example, you might define a module called my_module like this:

```
mod my_module {
    fn foo() {
        // ...
    }
}
```

You can then use the use keyword to bring the module into scope in your code:

```
use my_module;

fn main() {
    my_module::foo();
}
```

Modules can also be nested to create a hierarchy of modules. For example, you might define a module my_lib that contains several other modules:

```
mod my_lib {
    mod module_a {
        fn foo() {
            // ...
        }
    }
```

```rust
    mod module_b {
        fn bar() {
            // ...
        }
    }
}
```

To use a nested module, you can use the :: operator to specify the path to the module. Let's take a look at the following example:

```rust
use my_lib::module_a;

fn main() {
    module_a::foo();
}
```

Paths in Rust are used to specify the location of a module or other item in the module hierarchy. For example, the path `my_lib::module_a` specifies the location of the `module_a` module within the `my_lib` module.

Paths can also be used to specify the location of items within a module. For example, you might define a struct within a module like this:

```rust
mod my_module {
    struct MyStruct {
        // ...
    }
}
```

To refer to the MyStruct struct within the my_module module, you can use the path my_module::MyStruct.

Paths can be used in a variety of contexts in Rust, including in use statements, function calls, and more.

Accessing Cargo Packages

To access existing packages or crates on crates.io, the official Rust package registry, you can use the Cargo package manager.

To include a package or crate as a dependency in your Rust project, you can add it to the dependencies section of your Cargo.toml file. Let's take a look at the following example:

```
[dependencies]
my-crate = "0.1.0"
```

This will include the my-crate crate as a dependency in your project, and Cargo will automatically download and build the crate when you build your project.

You can also use the cargo search command to search for packages or crates on crates.io. Let's take a look at the following example:

```
cargo search my-crate
```

This will search for packages or crates on crates.io that match the search term "my-crate".

CHAPTER 8: CARGO COMMANDS

General and Build Commands

There are several common commands that you might use when working with Rust projects:

- **cargo new**: The cargo new command creates a new Rust project and generates the necessary files and directories for you. You can use it to create a new crate or package in Rust.

- **cargo build**: The cargo build command builds a Rust project and its dependencies, and creates a compiled version of the project. You can use it to build a crate or package in Rust.

- **cargo run**: The cargo run command builds and runs a Rust project. It is a convenient way to build and run a Rust project in one step.

- **cargo test**: The cargo test command runs the tests for a Rust project. It is a convenient way to run the tests for a Rust project and see the test results.

- **cargo doc**: The cargo doc command generates documentation for a Rust project and its dependencies. It creates an HTML version of the documentation that you can view in a web browser.

- **cargo publish**: The cargo publish command packages a Rust project and its dependencies, and publishes the package to the official Rust package registry, crates.io. This makes the package available for other users to include as a dependency in their own projects.

- **cargo update**: The cargo update command updates the dependencies of a Rust project to their latest versions. This can be useful if you want to update the dependencies of your project to the latest stable versions.

- **cargo clean**: The cargo clean command removes the compiled artifacts (such as executable files and object files) for a Rust project. This can be useful if you want to start a fresh build of your project.

- **cargo check**: The cargo check command performs a quick check of a Rust project to verify that it builds without actually building it. This can be useful if you want to verify that your project builds without actually building it.

- **cargo fmt**: The cargo fmt command reformats the source code of a Rust project according to the Rust formatting guidelines. This can be useful if you want to ensure that your code is consistently formatted.

- **cargo clippy**: The cargo clippy command is a linter for Rust projects. It checks the source code of your project for common mistakes and suggests improvements. This can be useful if you want to improve the quality and reliability of your code.

- **cargo install**: The cargo install command installs a Rust binary crate as a command-line utility. This can be useful if you want to install and use a Rust utility from the command line.

- **cargo tree**: The cargo tree command displays the dependencies of a Rust project as a tree. This can be useful if you want to see the dependencies of your project and how they are organized.

Manifest Commands

The manifest is a file called Cargo.toml that contains information about a Rust project or crate, including its name, version, dependencies, and more. The manifest is used by the Cargo package manager to manage and build the project.

There are several manifest-related commands that you might use when working with Rust projects:

- **cargo new**: The cargo new command creates a new Rust project and generates the necessary files and directories, including the manifest file.

- **cargo init**: The cargo init command creates a new manifest file for an existing Rust project.

- **cargo read-manifest**: The cargo read-manifest command reads the manifest file for a Rust project and prints its contents to the console.

- **cargo update**: The cargo update command updates the dependencies listed in the manifest file to their latest versions.

- **cargo tree**: The cargo tree command displays the dependencies of a Rust project as a tree, based on the information in the manifest file.

Package and Publish Commands

There are several package-related commands that you might use when working with Rust projects:

- **cargo package**: The cargo package command creates a package for a Rust project and its dependencies. The package is a tarball (a compressed archive file) that contains the source code and metadata for the project.

- **cargo publish**: The cargo publish command packages a Rust project and its dependencies, and publishes the package to the official Rust package registry, crates.io. This makes the package available for other users to include as a dependency in their own projects.

- **cargo install**: The cargo install command installs a Rust binary crate as a command-line utility. This can be useful if you want to install and use a Rust utility from the command line.

- **cargo search**: The cargo search command searches for packages or crates on crates.io that match a given search term. This can be useful if you want to find packages or crates that are available on crates.io.

Custom Commands

You can define custom commands to automate tasks or perform additional functionality in your projects. Custom commands are defined in the [package.metadata.cargo-script] section of the manifest file, Cargo.toml.

Following is an example of how to define a custom command in Rust:

```
[package.metadata.cargo-script]
my-command = "src/my_command.rs"
```

This defines a custom command called my-command, which is implemented in the src/my_command.rs file. to run the command, you can use the cargo script command:

```
cargo script my-command
```

Custom commands can be useful for automating tasks such as building, testing, and releasing your project. They can also be used to perform additional functionality beyond what is provided by the standard Cargo commands.

Each custom command is defined by a key-value pair, where the key is the name of the command and the value is the path to the script file that implements the command.

Following is an example of how to define multiple custom commands in Rust:

```
[package.metadata.cargo-script]
my-command = "src/my_command.rs"
my-other-command = "src/my_other_command.rs"
```

To run a custom command, you can use the cargo script command followed by the name of the command. Let's take a look at the following example:

```
cargo script my-command
cargo script my-other-command
```

Custom commands can be implemented in any script language that is supported by Cargo, such as Rust, Python, or Bash.

In the script file, you can use the cargo command to execute any of the standard Cargo commands, as well as any additional functionality that you want to include in the custom command.

For example, you might define a custom command that builds and releases your project, like this:

```bash
#!/usr/bin/env bash

cargo build --release
cargo package
cargo publish
```

Custom commands can be useful for automating tasks such as building, testing, and releasing your project. They can also be used to perform additional functionality beyond what is provided by the standard Cargo commands.

CHAPTER 9: USING RUST STANDARD LIBRARY

Overview

The Rust Standard Library is the collection of modules and functions that are included with the Rust programming language by default. It provides a wide range of functionality, including basic data types, file I/O, networking, and concurrency.

The Rust Standard Library is divided into a number of modules, each of which provides a specific set of functionality. Some of the most commonly used modules include:

- **std::collections**: This module provides data structures for storing and manipulating collections of data, such as vectors, linked lists, and hash maps.

- **std::error**: This module defines types and functions for handling errors that may occur during the execution of a Rust program.

- **std::fs**: This module provides functions for working with the file system, such as reading and writing files and creating, deleting, and renaming directories.

- **std::io**: This module provides functions for reading and writing data to and from various sources, such as the standard input and output streams and files.

- **std::net**: This module provides functions for working with network sockets and other networking functionality.

- **std::sync**: This module provides types and functions for working with concurrent programming, such as mutexes and atomic variables.

- **std::time**: This module provides types and functions for working with time and dates, such as measuring elapsed time and parsing and formatting dates and times.

In addition to these core modules, the Rust Standard Library also includes a number of other modules that provide a wide range of functionality, including math, strings, and utilities for working with the operating system.

One of the benefits of the Rust Standard Library is that it is designed to be efficient and safe, with a focus on ensuring that programs are free of common programming errors such as null or dangling pointer references. It is also well-documented, with detailed documentation available for each module and function in the library.

Std::Collections

The below example demonstrates how to use the std::collections::HashMap module to create a hash map, which is a data structure that allows you to store key-value pairs. The example inserts some key-value pairs into the hash map and then iterates over them, printing each name and score.

```
use std::collections::HashMap;

fn main() {
    let mut scores = HashMap::new();

    scores.insert("Alice", 10);
    scores.insert("Bob", 3);
    scores.insert("Charlie", 5);

    for (name, score) in &scores {
        println!("{}: {}", name, score);
    }
}
```

Std::Error

This example demonstrates how to use the std::error and std::fs modules to read the contents of a file. The read_file function uses the fs::read_to_string function to read the contents of the file and returns a Result type, which is an enum that can either be Ok with a value or Err with an error. The ? operator is used to propagate the error if one occurs. The unwrap function is used to get the value out of the Result, which will panic if the Result is an Err.

```
use std::error::Error;
use std::fs;
```

```
fn read_file(filename: &str) -> Result<String, Box<dyn
Error>> {
    let contents = fs::read_to_string(filename)?;
    Ok(contents)
}

fn main() {
    let contents = read_file("my_file.txt").unwrap();
    println!("{}", contents);
}
```

Std::Net

This example demonstrates how to use the std::net module to create a simple HTTP server.
The TcpListener type is used to bind to a particular IP address and port and listen for
incoming connections. The incoming method returns an iterator over the incoming
connections, and the TcpStream type represents a stream of data over a TCP connection.
The example reads data from the stream using the read method and writes a response using
the write and flush methods.

```
use std::net::{TcpListener, TcpStream};
use std::io::{Read, Write};

fn main() {
    let listener =
TcpListener::bind("127.0.0.1:8080").unwrap();

    for stream in listener.incoming() {
        let mut stream = stream.unwrap();

        let mut buf = [0; 1024];
        stream.read(&mut buf).unwrap();

        let response = "HTTP/1.1 200 OK\r\n\r\nHello,
world!";
        stream.write(response.as_bytes()).unwrap();
        stream.flush().unwrap();
```

Std::Sync

This example demonstrates how to use the `std::sync` module to safely share data between threads. The `Arc` type (short for "atomic reference count") is used to create a reference-counted pointer to the data, and the `Mutex` type is used to wrap the data in a mutual exclusion lock, which allows only one thread to access the data at a time. The `clone` method is used to create a copy of the `Arc`, which increases the reference count. The `lock` method is used to acquire the lock and get a mutable reference to the data. The `join` method is used to wait for the threads to finish.

```rust
use std::sync::{Arc, Mutex};
use std::thread;

fn main() {
    let data = Arc::new(Mutex::new(0));

    let data_clone = data.clone();
    let handle = thread::spawn(move || {
        let mut data = data_clone.lock
```



```rust
continue
.unwrap();
*data += 1;
});


let data_clone = data.clone();
let handle2 = thread::spawn(move || {
    let mut data = data_clone.lock().unwrap();
    *data += 1;
});
```

```rust
handle.join().unwrap();
handle2.join().unwrap();

println!("{}", data.lock().unwrap());
}
```

Std::Time

This example demonstrates how to use the `std::time` module to measure elapsed time. The `SystemTime` type represents a point in time relative to the system's epoch (the UNIX epoch is commonly used as the system's epoch). The `duration_since` method is used to calculate the duration between the current time and the epoch, and the `as_millis` method is used to convert the duration to milliseconds.

```rust
use std::time::{SystemTime, UNIX_EPOCH};

fn main() {
let start = SystemTime::now();
let since_the_epoch = start
.duration_since(UNIX_EPOCH)
.expect("Time went backwards");
let in_ms = since_the_epoch.as_millis();
println!("{}", in_ms);
}
```

Std::Env

This example demonstrates how to use the std::env module to get the command-line arguments passed to a program. The args method returns an iterator over the arguments, and the collect method is used to turn the iterator into a Vec of Strings.

```rust
use std::env;

fn main() {
```

```
    let args: Vec<String> = env::args().collect();
    println!("{:?}", args);
}
```

Std::Fmt

This example demonstrates how to use the std::fmt module to implement custom formatting for a struct. The fmt::Display trait is used to specify how the struct should be formatted when passed to the println! macro or other formatting functions. The fmt method takes a reference to the struct and a mutable reference to a fmt::Formatter and returns a fmt::Result. The write! macro is used to write the formatted output to the formatter.

```
use std::fmt;

struct Point {
    x: i32,
    y: i32,
}

impl fmt::Display for Point {
    fn fmt(&self, f: &mut fmt::Formatter<'_>) ->
fmt::Result {
        write!(f, "({}, {})", self.x, self.y)
    }
}

fn main() {
    let p = Point { x: 3, y: 4 };
    println!("{}", p);
}
```

Std::Str

This example demonstrates how to use the std::str module to convert a byte slice into a string. The from_utf8 function takes a byte slice and returns a Result containing either a string or an error if the slice is not valid UTF-8. The unwrap function is used to get the string out of the Result.

```
use std::str;

fn main() {
    let bytes = [104, 101, 108, 108, 111];
    let s = str::from_utf8(&bytes).unwrap();
    println!("{}", s);
}
```

Std::Iter

This example demonstrates how to use the std::iter module to create a vector of repeated values. The repeat function creates an iterator that infinitely repeats a value, and the take function limits the number of values produced by the iterator. The collect function is used to turn the iterator into a Vec.

```
use std::iter;

fn main() {
    let v: Vec<i32> =
iter::repeat(5).take(10).collect();
    println!("{:?}", v);
}
```

Std::Ops

This example demonstrates how to use the std::ops module to overload the + operator for a custom struct. The Add trait is implemented for the Point struct, and the add method is defined to specify how the + operator should behave for Points. The Output associated type is used to specify the type returned by the add method.

```rust
use std::ops::Add;

#[derive(Debug, PartialEq)]
struct Point {
    x: i32,
    y: i32,
}

impl Add for Point {
    type Output = Point;

    fn add(self, other: Point) -> Point {
        Point {
            x: self.x + other.x,
            y: self.y + other.y,
        }
    }
}

fn main() {
    let p1 = Point { x: 3, y: 4 };
    let p2 = Point { x: 5, y: 6 };
    let p3 = p1 + p2;
    assert_eq!(p3, Point { x: 8, y: 10 });
}
```

Std::Fs

This example demonstrates how to use the std::io module to read the contents of a file into a string. The File type is used to open the file, and the BufReader type is used to wrap the file in a buffer, which can improve performance when reading from the file. The read_to_string method is used to read the contents of the file into a string. The ? operator is used to propagate any errors that occur. The Result type is returned from the main function to indicate whether the operation was successful.

```rust
use std::fs::File;
```

```rust
use std::io::BufReader;
use std::io::prelude::*;

fn main() -> std::io::Result<()> {
    let file = File::open("my_file.txt")?;
    let mut reader = BufReader::new(file);
    let mut contents = String::new();
    reader.read_to_string(&mut contents)?;
    println!("{}", contents);
    Ok(())
}
```

Primitive Types

Primitive types are basic data types that are built into the language and are not represented as objects. They are typically more efficient to use than objects because they do not require the overhead of allocation on the heap or the use of reference counting.

Here are some of the primitive types in Rust:

- **bool**: a boolean type that can have one of two values: true or false.

- **char**: a character type that represents a Unicode scalar value, which is a single Unicode code point.

- **i8, i16, i32, i64, i128**: Integer types with signed two's complement representation, with 8, 16, 32, 64, and 128 bits of precision, respectively.

- **u8, u16, u32, u64, u128**: Integer types with unsigned representation, with 8, 16, 32, 64, and 128 bits of precision, respectively.

- **f32, f64**: Floating-point types with single and double precision, respectively.

- **usize, isize**: Integer types with unsigned and signed representation, respectively, that depend on the platform's pointer size.

Primitive types are commonly used in Rust for storing and manipulating basic data, such as numbers and Booleans. For example, you might use an i32 to store an integer value or a bool to store a truth value. You can also use primitive types as the basis for more complex data structures, such as arrays and slices.

Following is an example of how you might use some primitive types in Rust:

```rust
fn main() {
    let x: i32 = 5;
    let y: f64 = 3.14;
    let z: bool = true;
    let c: char = 'a';

    println!("x = {}", x);
    println!("y = {}", y);
    println!("z = {}", z);
    println!("c = {}", c);
}
```

In the given example, the variables x, y, z, and c are declared with the let keyword and are initialized with values of the i32, f64, bool, and char types, respectively. The values are then printed using the println! macro.

Let's take a look at another example of how you might use some more advanced features of primitive types in Rust:

```rust
fn main() {
    let x: i32 = 5;
    let y: f64 = 3.14;

    let z = x + y as i32;
    println!("z = {}", z);

    let a = [1, 2, 3, 4, 5];
    println!("a[2] = {}", a[2]);
    println!("a.len() = {}", a.len());
```

```
    let b = &a[1..3];
    println!("b = {:?}", b);
}
```

In the given example, the variable z is initialized with the result of adding an i32 and a f64. The as keyword is used to cast the f64 value to an i32 so that it can be added to the i32 value.

The a variable is an array of i32 values, and the b variable is a slice of a, which is a reference to a portion of the array. The [start..end] syntax is used to create the slice, which includes the elements at indices start through end - 1. The len method is used to get the length of the array, and the :? format specifier is used to print the slice in a debug format.

Primitive types are an important part of Rust's type system and are widely used in Rust programs for storing and manipulating basic data. They are efficient, versatile, and play a central role in many of the language's core features and data structures.

Collections

Collections are data structures that store and organize data in various ways. There are several types of collections in the Rust Standard Library, including arrays, vectors, slices, strings, and various types of maps and sets.

- Arrays are fixed-size collections of values of the same type. They are allocated on the stack and are indexed by integers. Let's take a look at the following example:

```
let a = [1, 2, 3, 4, 5];
let x = a[2];
```

- Vectors are growable arrays that are allocated on the heap. They can be resized to accommodate more elements and can be indexed by integers. Let's take a look at the following example:

```
let mut v = vec![1, 2, 3];
v.push(4);
let x = v[2];
```

- Slices are references to a portion of an array or vector. They do not own the data they reference and are commonly used to pass a portion of an array or vector to a function. Let's take a look at the following example:

```rust
let a = [1, 2, 3, 4, 5];
let s = &a[1..3];
```

- Strings are collections of Unicode characters that are stored as a contiguous sequence of bytes on the heap. They are represented by the String type, which is a growable, mutable string, and the str type, which is an immutable string slice. Let's take a look at the following example:

```rust
let mut s = String::from("hello");
s.push_str(", world");
let t: &str = "hello";
```

- Maps are collections of key-value pairs that are implemented as hash tables. They allow you to store and retrieve values by key. The HashMap type is a commonly used map that allows you to use any type that implements the Hash and Eq traits as a key. Let's take a look at the following example:

```rust
use std::collections::HashMap;

let mut scores = HashMap::new();
scores.insert("Alice", 10);
scores.insert("Bob", 3);
let score = scores.get("Alice");
```

- Sets are collections of unique values that are implemented as hash tables. They allow you to store and check for the presence of values without duplicates. The HashSet type is a commonly used set that allows you to use any type that implements the Hash and Eq traits as a value. Let's take a look at the following example:

```rust
use std::collections::HashSet;

let mut set = HashSet::new();
```

```rust
set.insert(1);
set.insert(2);
set.insert(2);
let contains = set.contains(&1);
```

These are just a few examples of the types of collections that are available in the Rust Standard Library. There are many more, each with its own specific characteristics and uses. Collections are an important part of Rust's standard library and are widely used for storing and organizing data in Rust

Macros

Macros are a way to generate code at compile time. They are defined using the macro_rules! macro and allow you to write code that looks like a function call, but which is expanded into a piece of code at compile time.

Macros are often used in Rust to create concise, reusable code that can be used to generate boilerplate or to perform complex tasks in a concise way. For example, the println! macro is used to print messages to the console and is defined as follows:

```rust
macro_rules! println {
    ($($arg:tt)*) => (print!("{}\n",
format_args!($($arg)*)))
}
```

The format_args! macro is used to format the arguments passed to the println! macro as a string, and the print! function is used to print the resulting string to the console.

Following is an example of how you might use the println! macro:

```rust
fn main() {
    println!("Hello, world!");
}
```

This will print the message "Hello, world!" to the console.

Macros can also be parameterized, which allows you to pass arguments to the macro and use them to generate code. For example, you might define a macro that generates a function with a specific name and body, like this:

```rust
macro_rules! define_function {
    ($name:ident, $body:expr) => {
        fn $name() {
            $body
        }
    }
}

define_function!(foo, println!("This is the body of the
foo function"));

fn main() {
    foo();
}
```

This will define a function called foo and call it in the main function. The $name:ident and $body:expr syntax is used to capture the arguments passed to the macro, and the $name and $body tokens are used to insert the values of the arguments into the generated code.

Macros are a powerful and flexible feature of Rust that can be used to generate code in a concise and reusable way. They are often used to create boilerplate code, perform complex tasks, and customize the behavior of the language.

Writing Your First Macro

To write your own macro with the name helpcode, you can use the macro_rules! macro, which is used to define Rust macros. Following is an example of how you might define a simple helpcode macro:

```rust
macro_rules! helpcode {
    () => {
        println!("For help with your code, try these
resources:");
```

```rust
        println!("- The Rust documentation:
https://doc.rust-lang.org/stable/");
        println!("- The Rust programming language book:
https://doc.rust-lang.org/stable/book/");
        println!("- The Rust reference:
https://doc.rust-lang.org/stable/reference/");
        println!("- Stack Overflow:
https://stackoverflow.com/");
        println!("- The Rust subreddit:
https://www.reddit.com/r/rust/");
    }
}
```

This macro defines a set of rules for the helpcode macro. The () => { ... } syntax is used to specify the body of the macro, which consists of a series of println! statements that print out a list of resources for getting help with Rust code.

To use the helpcode macro, you can simply call it like a function, like this:

```rust
fn main() {
    helpcode!();
}
```

This will expand the macro at compile time and print out the list of resources.

CHAPTER 10: MY FIRST COMMAND LINE APP (CLI)

Flowchart for Creating CLI Application

Below is a process flowchart for creating a command line application using Rust:

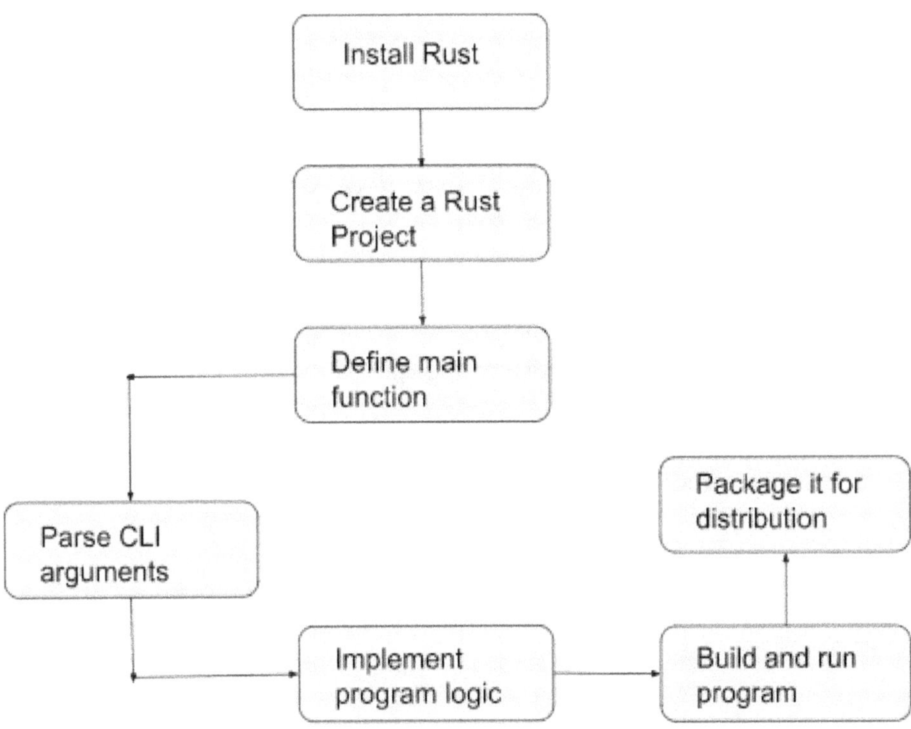

Procedure to Build CLI Aplication

Here's a step-by-step guide to creating a command line application using Rust:

Install Rust: The first step is to install the Rust programming language on your computer. You can do this by following the instructions given in chapter 2.

Create a new Rust project: Next, you'll need to create a new Rust project. You can do this using the cargo command-line tool, which is installed along with Rust. Run the following command to create a new project:

```
cargo new my-project
```

This will create a new directory called my-project with the necessary files for a Rust project.

Define main function: In Rust, the entry point for a command-line application is a function called main. You'll need to define this function in a file called main.rs.

Parse command-line arguments: In a command-line application, it's common to allow the user to pass in arguments when running the program. You can parse these arguments using the std::env::args function, which returns an iterator over the arguments passed to the program.

Implement your program's logic: Next, you'll need to implement the actual logic of your program. This will depend on what your program does, but could involve reading and writing files, making HTTP requests, or performing calculations.

Build and run your program: Once you've implemented the logic for your program, you can build and run it using the cargo tool. Run the following command to build your program:

```
cargo build
```

Then, you can run your program by running the following command:

```
cargo run
```

This will build and run your program, using the arguments you pass to the cargo run command as the arguments to your program.

(Optional) Package your program for distribution: If you want to distribute your program to other users, you can use the cargo tool to package it up into a binary file. Run the following command to build a binary file for your program:

```
cargo build --release
```

This will create a binary file for your program in the target/release directory. You can then distribute this binary file to other users, who can run it by simply running the file on the command line.

Building CLI App: File Sorting Program

Here's a step-by-step guide to creating a command-line application in Rust that sorts all files in a given directory by their modification dates:

First, create a new Rust project using the cargo command-line tool:

```
cargo new sort-files-by-date
```

Next, open the Cargo.toml file in the root of the project and add the following dependency:

```
[dependencies]
walkdir = "0.3.7"
```

The walkdir crate provides an easy-to-use iterator for recursively walking a directory tree. We'll use this to iterate over all the files in the given directory.

Next, open the src/main.rs file and import the walkdir and std::fs crates:

```
use std::fs;
use walkdir::WalkDir;
```

Add the following function to main.rs:

```
fn sort_files_by_date(dir: &str) {
    let mut entries: Vec<_> = WalkDir::new(dir)
        .into_iter()
        .filter_map(Result::ok)
        .filter(|e| e.file_type().is_file())
        .collect();
```

```rust
    entries.sort_by(|a, b| {
        let a_metadata =
fs::metadata(a.path()).unwrap();
        let b_metadata =
fs::metadata(b.path()).unwrap();
        a_metadata.modified().unwrap().cmp(&b_metadata.
modified().unwrap())
    });

    for entry in entries {
        println!("{}", entry.path().display());
    }
}
```

This function takes a directory path as a string and sorts all the files in the directory (and its subdirectories) by their modification dates. It does this by using the WalkDir iterator to recursively walk the directory tree, filtering out any non-file entries, and then sorting the resulting vector of file entries using the sort_by method and a comparison function that compares the modification dates of the files.

Finally, add the following code to the main function to parse the command-line arguments and call the sort_files_by_date function:

```rust
fn main() {
    let args: Vec<String> = std::env::args().collect();
    if args.len() != 2 {
        println!("Usage: sort-files-by-date
<directory>");
        std::process::exit(1);
    }

    let dir = &args[1];
    sort_files_by_date(dir);
}
```

This code parses the command-line arguments using the std::env::args function, which returns an iterator over the arguments passed to the program. It then checks that there are exactly two arguments (the program name and the directory path), and if not, prints a usage message and exits with an error code. Otherwise, it passes the directory path (the second argument) to the sort_files_by_date function.

That's it! You can now build and run the program using the following commands:

```
cargo build
./sort-
files-by-date <directory>
```

You can also use the `cargo run` command to build and run the program in one step:

```bash
cargo run <directory>
```

The program will output the paths of all the files in the given directory (and its subdirectories) sorted by their modification dates.

Lets look at how the output of the sort-files-by-date program might look:

```
$ cargo run testdir
testdir/file1.txt
testdir/subdir1/file2.txt
testdir/subdir1/file3.txt
testdir/subdir2/file4.txt
```

This shows the paths of all the files in the testdir directory sorted by their modification dates. In the given example, file1.txt has the oldest modification date, followed by file2.txt and file3.txt (which have the same modification date), and finally file4.txt, which has the newest modification date.

Note that the output includes the paths of files in subdirectories of the given directory as well. If you only want to sort the files in the top-level directory, you can modify the sort_files_by_date function to only include entries that have a depth of 1 (i.e., they are directly in the given directory). You can do this by adding a call to the depth method of the DirEntry struct before collecting the entries into the vector:

```rust
let mut entries: Vec<_> = WalkDir::new(dir)
    .into_iter()
    .filter_map(Result::ok)
    .filter(|e| e.file_type().is_file() && e.depth() ==
1)
    .collect();
```

This will only include entries that are directly in the given directory, rather than including entries in subdirectories as well.

To package this Rust program as a binary, you can use the cargo build --release command, which will build an optimized version of your program in the target/release directory. You can then distribute the binary file (e.g., sort-files-by-date on Linux or macOS, or sort-files-by-date.exe on Windows) to other users who can run it on their own systems.

If you want to publish your program to a package registry, such as crates.io, you'll need to create an account and follow the steps for publishing a crate. Here's a brief overview of the process:

- Run the cargo login command to log in to your crates.io account.
- Update the Cargo.toml file in your project to include a name and version field, as well as any other metadata you want to include (e.g., description, license, etc.).
- Run the cargo package command to build a tarball (.tar.gz) file containing your package.
- Run the cargo publish command to upload the tarball to crates.io.
- After publishing your package, other users will be able to include it as a dependency in their own Rust projects by adding it to the dependencies section of their Cargo.toml file:

```toml
[dependencies]
sort-files-by-date = "0.1.0"
```

They can then use your program by calling its functions in their own code.

CHAPTER 11: CODE TESTING OF APPLICATIONS

Types of Software Testing

Software testing is the process of finding errors in the developed product. It also checks whether the real outcomes can match expected results, as well as aids in the identification of defects, missing requirements, or gaps. Testing is the penultimate step before the launch of the product to the market. It includes examination, analysis, observation, and evaluation of different aspects of a product.

Software testing is the process of evaluating a software system or its components to determine whether it satisfies specified requirements and to identify any defects. There are several types of software testing, each with its own characteristics and goals. Some common types of software testing include:

- Unit testing: This type of testing involves testing individual units or components of a software system in isolation from the rest of the system. The goal of unit testing is to validate that each unit of the software system is working correctly on its own.

  Unit testing ensures that individual units or components of the software system are working correctly. By catching defects early in the development process, unit testing can save time and resources by reducing the need for debugging and fixing defects later in the development process. Unit testing also helps improve the quality of the software system by providing a high level of confidence that the individual units or components are working correctly.

- Integration testing: This type of testing involves testing the interaction between multiple units or components of a software system. The goal of integration testing is to validate that the units or components work together correctly.

  Integration testing confirms that the various units or components of a software system work together correctly. By catching defects that occur when different units or components interact, integration testing can help prevent issues from being discovered late in the development process, which can be more costly and time-consuming to fix.

- System testing: This type of testing involves testing the entire software system as a whole, including all its components and their interactions. The goal of system testing is to validate that the software system meets the specified requirements and functions as intended.

It verifies that the software system as a whole is functioning correctly and meets the specified requirements. By catching defects at this stage, system testing can help prevent issues from being discovered late in the development process or by end users, which can lead to user dissatisfaction and costly repairs.

- Acceptance testing: This type of testing involves testing the software system from the perspective of the end user. The goal of acceptance testing is to determine whether the software system is acceptable to the user and meets their needs.

  This particular testing checks that the software system is acceptable to the end user and meets their needs. By involving the end user in the testing process, acceptance testing can help ensure that the software system is fit for its intended purpose and meets the user's expectations.

- Regression testing: This type of testing involves re-testing the software system after changes have been made to ensure that the changes have not introduced any new defects or caused any existing functionality to break. The goal of regression testing is to validate that the software system is still working correctly after changes have been made.

  This test figures out that changes to the software system have not introduced any new defects or caused any existing functionality to break. By performing regression testing after changes have been made, it is possible to catch defects early and prevent them from causing issues later on.

- Performance testing: This type of testing involves evaluating the performance of the software system under different loads or conditions. The goal of performance testing is to determine the limits of the software system and identify any performance issues.

  With this testing. you can be rest assured that the software system is able to handle the expected load and perform at an acceptable level. By identifying performance issues early on, it is possible to optimize the software system and improve its overall performance.

Overall, the different types of software testing help improve the quality and reliability of a software system by catching defects early in the development process and ensuring that the software system meets the specified requirements and performs as expected.

Run Code Testing on CLI Application

In general, unit testing is a good choice for testing individual units or components of a software system in isolation from the rest of the system. This can be especially useful for testing small, self-contained units of code that have a clear input/output behavior.

Unit testing can be particularly useful for CLI applications because it allows you to test the individual functions or components of the application in isolation, without having to run the entire program. This can make it easier to identify and fix defects, and can also help ensure that the application is working correctly before integrating it with other components.

In Rust, you can use the assert_eq! macro from the assert_eq crate to perform unit testing on your code. to use this macro, you'll need to add the following to your Cargo.toml file:

```
[dev-dependencies]
assert_eq = "0.6.0"
```

Then, you can write test functions in your src/main.rs file using the #[test] attribute:

```rust
#[test]
fn test_sort_files_by_date() {
    let dir = "testdir";
    let expected_output = vec![
        "testdir/file1.txt",
        "testdir/subdir1/file2.txt",
        "testdir/subdir1/file3.txt",
        "testdir/subdir2/file4.txt",
    ];
    let mut output = Vec::new();

    sort_files_by_date(dir);
    for entry in WalkDir::new(dir) {
        output.push(entry.unwrap().path().display().to_
string());
    }
```

```
    assert_eq!(output, expected_output);
}
```

This test function calls the sort_files_by_date function on a test directory (testdir) and compares the resulting sorted list of file paths to an expected output using the assert_eq! macro. If the output does not match the expected output, the test will fail.

To run the tests, you can use the cargo test command:

```
cargo test
```

This will run all the test functions in your project and report the results.

You can also write integration tests that test the entire program by running it as an external process and comparing its output to expected output. to do this, you can use the std::process::Command struct from the std crate to run the program and capture its output, and then use the assert_eq! macro to compare the output to the expected output.

Let's take a look at the following example:

```
#[test]
fn test_cli() {
    let output = std::process::Command::new("./sort-
files-by-date")
        .arg("testdir")
        .output()
        .unwrap();
    let output_str =
String::from_utf8(output.stdout).unwrap();
    let expected_output_str =
"testdir/file1.txt\ntestdir/subdir1/file2.txt\ntestdir/
subdir1/file3.txt\ntestdir/subdir2/file4.txt\n";

    assert_eq!(output_str, expected_output_str);
}
```

This test function runs the sort-files-by-date program with the testdir argument.

Chapter 12: Smart Pointers & Reference Cycles

Understanding Smart Pointers

A smart pointer is a type that represents a pointer to some data, but which also has additional behavior or semantics associated with it. Smart pointers are used to manage the lifetime of data and to ensure that resources are properly released when they are no longer needed.

There are several types of smart pointers in Rust, including:

Box<T>: a type that represents a heap-allocated value. It is used to store a value on the heap and can be used to transfer ownership of the value without copying it.

Rc<T>: a type that represents a reference-counted value. It is used to share ownership of a value between multiple locations in a program and ensures that the value is not dropped until all references to it are dropped.

Arc<T>: a type that represents a reference-counted value that can be shared between threads. It is similar to Rc<T>, but it is thread-safe and can be used to share values between threads in a concurrent program.

Weak<T>: a type that represents a weak reference to a value stored in an Rc<T>. It does not increase the reference count of the value and is used to prevent reference cycles.

Box<T>

Box<T> is a smart pointer that represents a heap-allocated value. It is used to store a value on the heap and can be used to transfer ownership of the value without copying it.

Following is an example of how you might use the Box<T> smart pointer in Rust:

```rust
fn main() {
    let b = Box::new(5);
    println!("b = {}", b);
}
```

This example creates a Box<T> smart pointer that stores an i32 value on the heap. The Box::new function is used to allocate the value on the heap and create a Box<T> that points to it. The value can then be accessed through the Box<T> by dereferencing it with the * operator.

Let's take a look at another example of how you might use the Box<T> smart pointer to transfer ownership of a value:

```
fn main() {
    let a = 5;
    let b = Box::new(a);
    let c = *b;
    println!("a = {}, b = {}, c = {}", a, b, c);
}
```

In the given example, the Box::new function is used to create a Box<T> that stores the value of a on the heap. The value of a is then moved into the Box<T>, and the value of a is no longer accessible. The value can then be accessed through the Box<T> by dereferencing it with the * operator and assigning it to the variable c.

Lets look at one more example on how we might use the Box<T> smart pointer to store a data structure on the heap:

```
#[derive(Debug)]
struct Point {
    x: f64,
    y: f64,
}

fn main() {
    let p = Box::new(Point { x: 1.0, y: 2.0 });
    println!("p = {:?}", p);
}
```

In the given example, the Point struct represents a 2D point with x and y coordinates. The Box::new function is used to create a Box<T> that stores a Point value on the heap. The value can then be accessed through the Box<T> by dereferencing it with the * operator and printing it with the Debug trait, which is implemented for the Point struct.

Box<T> is a useful smart pointer when you want to store a data structure on the heap and manipulate it through a reference. It is lightweight and efficient, and it is often used in conjunction with other data structures and algorithms in Rust.

It is important to note that Box<T> does not implement the Copy trait, which means that values stored in a Box<T> are moved into the box and cannot be accessed directly after the move. This is an important feature of Box<T> that allows it to transfer ownership of the value without copying it. If you need to copy a value, you can use a different data structure, such as an array or a vector, or you can implement the Copy trait for your data structure.

Rc<T>

Rc<T> is a smart pointer that represents a reference-counted value. It is used to share ownership of a value between multiple locations in a program and ensures that the value is not dropped until all references to it are dropped.

Following is an example of how you might use the Rc<T> smart pointer in Rust:

```rust
use std::rc::Rc;

fn main() {
    let a = Rc::new(5);
    let b = a.clone();
    println!("a = {}, b = {}", a, b);
}
```

This example creates an Rc<T> smart pointer that stores an i32 value on the heap and shares it between two locations in the program. The Rc::new function is used to allocate the value on the heap and create an Rc<T> that points to it. The clone method is used to create a new reference to the value, which increases the reference count. The values can then be accessed through the Rc<T> smart pointers by dereferencing them with the * operator.

Let's take a look at another example of how you might use the Rc<T> smart pointer to share a data structure between multiple locations:

```rust
#[derive(Debug)]
struct Point {
    x: f64,
    y: f64,
}

fn main() {
    let p = Rc::new(Point { x: 1.0, y: 2.0 });
    let q = p.clone();
    println!("p = {:?}, q = {:?}", p, q);
}
```

In the given example, the Point struct represents a 2D point with x and y coordinates. The Rc::new function is used to create an Rc<T> that stores a Point value on the heap and shares it between two locations in the program. The clone method is used to create a new reference to the value, which increases the reference count. The values can then be accessed through the Rc<T> smart pointers by dereferencing them with the * operator and printing them with the Debug trait, which is implemented for the Point struct.

Rc<T> is a useful smart pointer when you want to share a value between multiple locations in a program and ensure that the value is not dropped until all references to it are dropped. It is lightweight and efficient, and it is often used in conjunction with other data structures and algorithms in Rust.

Arc<T>

Arc<T> is a smart pointer that represents a reference-counted value that can be shared between threads. It is similar to Rc<T>, but it is thread-safe and can be used to share values between threads in a concurrent program.

Following is an example of how you might use the Arc<T> smart pointer in Rust:

```rust
use std::sync::Arc;
use std::thread;

fn main() {
    let a = Arc::new(5);
```

```rust
    let b = a.clone();

    let handle = thread::spawn(move || {
        println!("a = {}, b = {}", a, b);
    });

    handle.join().unwrap();
}
```

This example creates an Arc<T> smart pointer that stores an i32 value on the heap and shares it between the main thread and a new thread that is spawned with the thread::spawn function. The Arc::new function is used to allocate the value on the heap and create an Arc<T> that points to it. The clone method is used to create a new reference to the value, which increases the reference count. The values can then be accessed through the Arc<T> smart pointers by dereferencing them with the * operator.

Let's take a look at another example of how you might use the Arc<T> smart pointer to share a data structure between threads:

```rust
use std::sync::Arc;
use std::thread;

#[derive(Debug)]
struct Point {
    x: f64,
    y: f64,
}

fn main() {
    let p = Arc::new(Point { x: 1.0, y: 2.0 });
    let q = p.clone();

    let handle = thread::spawn(move || {
        println!("p = {:?}, q = {:?}", p, q);
    });

    handle.join().unwrap();
```

}

In the given example, the Point struct represents a 2D point with x and y coordinates. The Arc::new function is used to create an Arc<T> that stores a Point value on the heap and shares it between the main thread and a new thread that is spawned with the thread::spawn function. The clone method is used to create a new reference to the value, which increases the reference count. The values can then be accessed through the Arc<T> smart pointers by dereferencing them with the * operator and printing them with the Debug trait, which is implemented for the Point struct.

Arc<T> is a useful smart pointer when you want to share a value between threads in a concurrent program and ensure that the value is not dropped until all references to it are dropped. It is thread-safe and efficient, and it is often used in conjunction with other data structures and algorithms in Rust.

Weak<T>

Weak<T> is a smart pointer that represents a weak reference to a value stored in an Rc<T>. It does not increase the reference count of the value and is used to prevent reference cycles.

Following is an example of how you might use the Weak<T> smart pointer in Rust:

```rust
use std::rc::{Rc, Weak};

struct Node {
    value: i32,
    parent: Weak<Node>,
    children: Vec<Rc<Node>>,
}

fn main() {
    let a = Rc::new(Node {
        value: 5,
        parent: Weak::new(),
        children: Vec::new(),
    });
    let b = Rc::new(Node {
```

```rust
        value: 6,
        parent: Rc::downgrade(&a),
        children: Vec::new(),
    });
    a.children.push(Rc::clone(&b));
}
```

In the given example, the Node struct represents a node in a tree data structure with a value, a parent node, and a vector of child nodes. The parent node is stored as a Weak<Node> smart pointer, which does not increase the reference count of the parent node. The child nodes are stored as Rc<Node> smart pointers, which do increase the reference count of the child nodes. The Rc::downgrade function is used to create a Weak<Node> reference to the parent node from an Rc<Node> reference, and the Rc::clone function is used to create a new Rc<Node> reference to the child node.

Let's take a look at another example of how you might use the Weak<T> smart pointer to prevent a reference cycle:

```rust
use std::rc::{Rc, Weak};

struct Node {
    value: i32,
    parent: Option<Rc<Node>>,
    children: Vec<Rc<Node>>,
}

fn main() {
    let a = Rc::new(Node {
        value: 5,
        parent: None,
        children: Vec::new(),
    });
    let b = Rc::new(Node {
        value: 6,
        parent: Some(Rc::downgrade(&a)),
        children: Vec::new(),
    });
```

```rust
        a.children.push(Rc::clone(&b));
}
```

In the given example, the Node struct represents a node in a tree data structure with a value, a parent node, and a vector of child nodes. The parent node is stored as an Option<Rc<Node>>, which allows it to be None if the node is the root of the tree. The child nodes are stored as Rc<Node> smart pointers, which increase the reference count of the child nodes. The Rc::downgrade function is used to create a Weak<Node> reference to the parent node from an Rc<Node> reference, and the Rc::clone function is used to create a new Rc<Node> reference to the child node. This prevents a reference cycle from forming, as the Weak<Node> reference to the parent node does not increase the reference count of the parent node.

Weak<T> is an important part of Rust's reference counting mechanism and is used to prevent reference cycles and ensure that values are dropped when they are no longer needed. It is lightweight and efficient, and it is often used in conjunction with other data structures and algorithms in Rust.

Understanding Reference Cycles

A reference cycle is a type of memory leak that occurs when two or more values hold references to each other in a circular manner, preventing the values from being dropped when they are no longer needed.

Following is an example of a reference cycle in Rust:

```rust
use std::rc::Rc;

struct Node {
    value: i32,
    parent: Rc<Node>,
    children: Vec<Rc<Node>>,
}

fn main() {
    let a = Rc::new(Node {
        value: 5,
```

```
                    parent: Rc::new(Node {
                        value: 6,
                        parent: Rc::new(Node {
                            value: 7,
                            parent: Rc::new(Node {
                                value: 8,
                                parent: Rc::new(Node {
                                    value: 9,
                                    parent: Rc::new(Node {
                                        value: 10,
                                        parent: Rc::new(Node {
                                            value: 11,
                                            parent: Rc::new(Node {
                                                value: 12,
                                                parent:
Rc::new(Node {
                                                    value: 13,
                                                    parent:
Rc::new(Node {
                                                        value: 14,
                                                        parent:
Rc::new(Node {
                                                            value:
15,
                                                            parent:
Rc::new(Node {
                                                                val
ue: 16,
                                                                par
ent: Rc::new(Node {

  value: 17,

  parent: Rc::new(Node {

    value: 18,
```

```rust
    parent: Rc::new(Node {

        value: 19,

        parent: Rc::new(Node {

            value: 20,

            parent: Rc::new(Node {

                value: 21,

                parent: Rc::new(Node {

                    value: 22,

                    parent: Rc::new(Node {

                        value: 23,

                        parent: Rc::new(Node {

                            value: 24,

                            parent: Rc::new(Node {

                                value: 25,

                                parent: Rc::new(Node {

                                    value: 26,

                                    parent:
Rc::new(Node {

                                        value: 27,
```

```
Rc::new(Node {

Rc::new(Node {

29,

: Rc::new(Node {

lue: 30,

rent: Rc::new(Node {

    value: 31,

    parent: Rc::new(Node {

        value: 32,

        parent: Rc::new(Node {

            value: 33,

                                parent:

                                        value: 28,

                                parent:

                                            value:

                                        parent

                                                va

                                            pa
```

Types of Reference Cycles

There are two main types of reference cycles in Rust:

- Reference cycles between objects: These occur when two or more objects hold references to each other in a circular manner, preventing the objects from being dropped when they are no longer needed. This type of reference cycle is common in data structures such as linked lists and trees, where nodes hold references to their parent and child nodes.

- Reference cycles between objects and closures: These occur when an object holds a reference to a closure that captures the object, creating a circular reference. This type of reference cycle is common when working with asynchronous tasks and event loops, where a closure is used to schedule a task to be executed at a later time.

Both types of reference cycles can cause memory leaks in a program, as the values are not dropped when they are no longer needed. to prevent reference cycles, you can use weak references or break the cycle by breaking the circular reference. Weak references, such as Weak<T>, do not increase the reference count of the value and are used to prevent reference cycles without preventing the value from being dropped when it is no longer needed. Breaking the circular reference involves modifying the data structure or closure to avoid the circular reference.

Creating a Reference Cycle: Between Objects

To create a reference cycle between objects in Rust, you can create two or more objects that hold references to each other in a circular manner. Following is an example of a reference cycle between two objects:

```rust
use std::rc::Rc;

struct Node {
    value: i32,
    parent: Rc<Node>,
    children: Vec<Rc<Node>>,
}
```

```rust
fn main() {
    let a = Rc::new(Node {
        value: 5,
        parent: Rc::new(Node {
            value: 6,
            parent: Rc::new(Node {
                value: 7,
                parent: Rc::new(Node {
                    value: 8,
                    parent: Rc::new(Node {
                        value: 9,
                        parent: Rc::new(Node {
                            value: 10,
                            parent: Rc::new(Node {
                                value: 11,
                                parent: Rc::new(Node {
                                    value: 12,
                                    parent:
Rc::new(Node {
                                        value: 13,
                                        parent:
Rc::new(Node {
                                            value: 14,
                                            parent:
Rc::new(Node {
                                                value:
15,
                                                parent:
Rc::new(Node {
                                                    val
ue: 16,
                                                    par
ent: Rc::new(Node {

  value: 17,

  parent: Rc::new(Node {
```

```rust
        value: 18,

        parent: Rc::new(Node {

            value: 19,

            parent: Rc::new(Node {

                value: 20,

                parent: Rc::new(Node {

                    value: 21,

                    parent: Rc::new(Node {

                        value: 22,

                        parent: Rc::new(Node {

                            value: 23,

                            parent: Rc::new(Node {

                                value: 24,

                                parent: Rc::new(Node {

                                    value: 25,

                                    parent: Rc::new(Node {

                                        value: 26,

                                        parent:
Rc::new(Node {
```

```
value: 27,

parent:

Rc::new(Node {

value: 28,

parent:

Rc::new(Node {

value:
29,

parent

: Rc::new(Node {

...
```

In the given example, the Node struct represents a node in a tree data structure with a value, a parent node, and a vector of child nodes. The parent node is stored as an Rc<Node> smart pointer, which increases the reference count of the parent node. The child nodes are also stored as Rc<Node> smart pointers, which increase the reference count of the child nodes. This creates a reference cycle between the nodes, as the parent node holds a reference to the child node.

Reference cycles between objects can be useful in certain cases, such as when implementing data structures that require circular references. For example, a linked list is a data structure that consists of a sequence of nodes, where each node holds a value and a reference to the next node in the list. a circular linked list is a variation of a linked list where the last node in the list holds a reference to the first node, creating a circular reference.

Following is an example of a circular linked list in Rust:

```rust
use std::rc::Rc;

struct Node {
    value: i32,
    next: Option<Rc<Node>>,
```

```rust
}

fn main() {
    let a = Rc::new(Node {
        value: 5,
        next: None,
    });
    let b = Rc::new(Node {
        value: 6,
        next: Some(Rc::clone(&a)),
    });
    let c = Rc::new(Node {
        value: 7,
        next: Some(Rc::clone(&b)),
    });
    a.next = Some(Rc::clone(&c));
}
```

In the given example, the Node struct represents a node in the linked list with a value and a reference to the next node. The next field is an Option<Rc<Node>> that allows it to be None if the node is the last node in the list. The reference cycle is created by setting the next field of the first node to the last node, and the next field of the last node to the first node.

Reference cycles between objects can be useful for implementing data structures that require circular references, but they can also cause memory leaks if not properly managed. to prevent reference cycles, you can use weak references or break the cycle by breaking the circular reference. Weak references, such as Weak<T>, do not increase the reference count of the value and are used to prevent reference cycles without preventing the value from being dropped when it is no longer needed. Breaking the circular reference involves modifying the data structure to avoid the circular reference.

Creating a Reference Cycle: Between Objects & Closure

To create a reference cycle between an object and a closure in Rust, you can create an object that holds a reference to a closure that captures the object, creating a circular reference. Following is an example of a reference cycle between an object and a closure:

```rust
use std::rc::Rc;

struct Task {
    value: i32,
    callback: Box<dyn Fn() + 'static>,
}

fn main() {
    let a = Rc::new(Task {
        value: 5,
        callback: Box::new(move || {
            println!("a = {:?}", a);
        }),
    });
}
```

In the given example, the Task struct represents a task with a value and a callback closure. The closure captures the Task object and is stored in the callback field as a boxed trait object. This creates a reference cycle between the Task object and the closure, as the Task object holds a reference to the closure, and the closure captures the Task object.

Reference cycles between objects and closures can be useful in certain cases, such as when working with asynchronous tasks and event loops. For example, you can use a reference cycle to schedule a task to be executed at a later time by creating a closure that captures the task and adding it to an event loop. The event loop can then execute the closure at the appropriate time, allowing the task to be performed asynchronously.

Following is an example of using a reference cycle to schedule a task to be executed asynchronously:

```rust
use std::rc::Rc;
use std::time::Duration;

struct Task {
    value: i32,
    callback: Box<dyn Fn() + 'static>,
```

```rust
}

fn main() {
    let a = Rc::new(Task {
        value: 5,
        callback: Box::new(move || {
            println!("a = {:?}", a);
        }),
    });
    let event_loop = EventLoop::new();
    event_loop.schedule(Duration::from_secs(5),
Rc::clone(&a));
}
```

In the given example, the Task struct represents a task with a value and a callback closure. The event_loop object represents an event loop that can schedule tasks to be executed at a later time. The schedule method adds the task to the event loop and schedules it to be executed after a given duration.

Weak references, such as Weak<T>, do not increase the reference count of the value and are used to prevent reference cycles without preventing the value from being dropped when it is no longer needed. You can use weak references in a closure by creating a weak reference to the object inside the closure, and then using the upgrade method to convert it back to a strong reference when needed.

Following is an example of using a weak reference to prevent a reference cycle between an object and a closure:

```rust
use std::rc::{Rc, Weak};

struct Task {
    value: i32,
    callback: Box<dyn Fn() + 'static>,
}

fn main() {
    let a = Rc::new(Task {
        value: 5,
```

```rust
        callback: Box::new(move || {
            let a = a.upgrade().unwrap();
            println!("a = {:?}", a);
        }),
    });
    let weak_a = Rc::downgrade(&a);
    a.callback = Box::new(move || {
        let a = weak_a.upgrade().unwrap();
        println!("a = {:?}", a);
    });
}
```

In the given example, the Task struct represents a task with a value and a callback closure. The a variable is a strong reference to the Task object, and the weak_a variable is a weak reference to the same object. The first closure captures the strong reference to the Task object and creates a reference cycle. to prevent the reference cycle, the second closure captures the weak reference to the Task object instead. The upgrade method is used to convert the weak reference back to a strong reference when it is needed inside the closure.

Another way to prevent reference cycles is to break the cycle by breaking the circular reference. This involves modifying the data structure or closure to avoid the circular reference. For example, in the linked list example, you can break the reference cycle by changing the next field from an Option<Rc<Node>> to an Option<Box<Node>>. This allows the nodes to be dropped when they are no longer needed, as the reference count of a Box is not incremented when it is cloned.

Preventing Reference Cycles

To prevent reference cycles in Rust, you can use weak references or break the cycle by breaking the circular reference.

Weak references, such as Weak<T>, do not increase the reference count of the value and are used to prevent reference cycles without preventing the value from being dropped when it is no longer needed. You can use weak references in a closure by creating a weak reference to the object inside the closure, and then using the upgrade method to convert it back to a strong reference when needed.

Following is an example of using a weak reference to prevent a reference cycle between an object and a closure:

```rust
use std::rc::{Rc, Weak};

struct Task {
    value: i32,
    callback: Box<dyn Fn() + 'static>,
}

fn main() {
    let a = Rc::new(Task {
        value: 5,
        callback: Box::new(move || {
            let a = a.upgrade().unwrap();
            println!("a = {:?}", a);
        }),
    });
    let weak_a = Rc::downgrade(&a);
    a.callback = Box::new(move || {
        let a = weak_a.upgrade().unwrap();
        println!("a = {:?}", a);
    });
}
```

In the given example, the Task struct represents a task with a value and a callback closure. The a variable is a strong reference to the Task object, and the weak_a variable is a weak reference to the same object. The first closure captures the strong reference to the Task object and creates a reference cycle. to prevent the reference cycle, the second closure captures the weak reference to the Task object instead. The upgrade method is used to convert the weak reference back to a strong reference when it is needed inside the closure.

Another way to prevent reference cycles is to break the cycle by breaking the circular reference. This involves modifying the data structure or closure to avoid the circular reference. For example, in the linked list example, you can break the reference cycle by changing the next field from an Option<Rc<Node>> to an Option<Box<Node>>. This allows the nodes to be dropped when they are no longer needed, as the reference count of a Box is not incremented when it is cloned.

Thank You